MW00571706

ADVANCE PRAISE

"With sensitivity, love, and humor, Emanuel Rosen tells the story of his Yekke grandparents, their immigration and difficulties in the homeland of the Jewish people, and their journey in search of their roots and identity in Germany. An important and fascinating book that awakened in me deep feelings and a longing for a generation that is no more."

Gabriela Shalev: *former Israel's Ambassador to the U.N.; Professor (Emeritus) the Hebrew University of Jerusalem*

"I thought I'd take a quick look at this book, but then I kept reading all of it in a day and a half."

W. Michael Blumenthal: *Former U.S. Secretary of the Treasury and director of the Jewish Museum Berlin (1997-2014)*

"From generation to generation, it becomes more difficult to write about the persecution of Jews before and during WWII as one's personal past. Too much has been lost, and precisely because of that one wants to write about what can still be found. I respect what Emanuel Rosen did in this book, patiently and carefully exploring the past and guiding us through his findings about the story of his family."

Bernhard Schlink: *Author of "The Reader"*

"This is a gripping and engaging exploration of a family whose lives were indelibly changed by Nazi restrictions, by immigrant life in Israel, and by a grandson's search for missing parts of the stories."

Martha Minow: *Harvard Law School*

"The mystery of why Emanuel Rosen's grandfather killed himself haunts this book and keeps the reader gripped until the secrets of the past are ultimately uncovered and revealed. Suicide leaves a legacy of silence for those of us who are left behind and works such as this allows us to begin to understand how we are affected and start to heal. This book will greatly help survivors of suicide loss on their own personal journeys of discovery and hope."

Carla Fine: Author of "No Time to Say Goodbye: Surviving the Suicide of a Loved One"

IF ANYONE CALLS, TELL THEM I DIED

A MEMOIR

EMANUEL (MANU) ROSEN

ISBN: 9789493231146 (ebook)
ISBN: 9789493231139 (paperback)
ISBN: 9789493231283 (hardcover)

Cover: Mirjam Rosen typing at home in summer 1957.

Copyright © 2021 Emanuel (Manu) Rosen

Publisher: Amsterdam Publishers

info@amsterdampublishers.com

Holocaust Survivor True Stories WWII, Book 9

CONTENTS

To immigrants and the uprooted

1 TEL AVIV

"IT'S NOT FUNNY TO ME."

My mom hardly ever told a joke, but she had one-liners ready for any occasion. If you told her that somebody was getting married, she would shoot back, "Against whom?" Before she would take her afternoon nap, she would order, "If anyone calls, tell them I died." If we saw an ugly piece of art in a shopping window, she would warn my sister and me, "If you don't behave, I'll buy this one for you!" And if she talked about us with a neighbor or a relative, she would sum it up, "They're good kids." And after a well-timed two-second pause she'd add, "Especially when they're asleep."

As opposed to her pre-packaged humor, I loved telling new jokes, and growing up, she participated—patiently, I should say—in the different phases of joke telling I experimented with. When I was a teenager in the 1960s, my friends and I were obsessed for a while with what we called "horror jokes," and I would get special pleasure telling these jokes to my mom because of the mix of laughter and moaning they would invoke in her. Jokes such as "Did you hear about the blind man who bled to death trying to read a cheese grater?" She would put her hands over her glasses, shake her head, and say, "This is awful!" or "Enough!" But she would still be laughing.

One day, another boy at school told me a new joke, "You know that falling from a tall building won't kill you?"

This sounded promising. I waited for the punch line.

"It's the contact with the sidewalk that does the trick."

I thought it was hilarious. Back from school, I couldn't wait to tell my mom the new joke. When I heard her car approaching, I waited for her in the "hall", a pretentious name for the little corridor that connected the three rooms of the house. When she came in, I told her I had a new joke, "You know that falling from a tall building won't kill you?"

My mom froze. Her lips twitched for a second, and her grey eyes didn't move.

"It's the contact with the sidewalk that does the trick."

She turned away. "It's not funny," she said, her gaze fixated on the blue armchair by the phone.

I insisted that it was a funny joke. A *very* funny joke. How couldn't she see that it was funny?

"It's not funny to me."[1]

2 MENLO PARK
"THIS IS NOT FOR THE CAR."

I found a bunch of letters in an old box that I had brought from my mom's house in Tel Aviv after she had died. A bunch of letters that had survived decades of clean-ups had to be important, but between my poor German and the old-fashioned handwriting they were written in, I couldn't figure out why. Now I was a man with a family, older than my mom was when I was a stupid teenager. I was busy living life, yet once in a while, I would open up that box and give it another try. Something pulled me to these letters that held the answer to a question I didn't know I had.

They were written by my grandparents, Dr. Hugo Mendel, whom we called Opa (grandpa in German) and Lucie Mendel, whom we called Oma (grandma), on a trip they had taken to Germany in 1956, and most were addressed to Mirjam or Mirjämchen, a term of endearment they used to call my mom. And then one day, the question that these letters could answer became clear. My grandparents separated after that trip, and I realized that these letters could explain why. By "separated," I don't mean that they divorced but that each went his and her own way. My grandma decided to live, and my grandpa decided to die.[1]

Their return to Israel from this trip to Germany is one of my first memories. It was in October 1956, I was three and a half, and I remember standing by the table we called "the short table," which at the time stood at my eye level. Except for the table itself, I remember two things: A few blurred figures in the background and one present they had brought back from Germany—a green bath sponge in the shape of an elephant. I don't think I've ever been happier with a present. It thrilled me beyond measure—a sponge that's also an elephant! In Tel Aviv of the 1950s, things did not tend to be in the shape of other things—a sponge was a sponge, and an elephant was an elephant, and suddenly this? I vaguely remember the blurred figures laughing at my uncontrolled excitement.

All my memories are from the years that followed that trip, and I remember them as happy ones. I had an uncle named Raphi, a tall and handsome man who knew how to wiggle his ears. I had a mother who was the fastest typist in the world and knew how to spit amazing distances. To this day, I haven't met a better spitter. There was Tante Liese (Aunt Liese, my grandfather Hugo's sister), round and short, who always looked like she had just woken up and who would crack me up by hanging cherries on her ears like earrings. And there was Oma (my grandma Lucie), a tall woman with a Margaret Thatcher hairdo, who knew how to blow a blade of grass she would put between her thumbs to produce ridiculously loud trumpet sounds.

It was a women's tribe. My uncle Raphi was usually abroad, my grandfather Hugo, as mentioned, had decided to die, and my father had died of a heart attack when I was eight months old. I, the only male present, was a loyal member of this mini-tribe. Today, I know that the memory of the two dead men—my father and grandfather —was always hovering over us, but as a child, I was oblivious to that, and I was captured by the magic of the tribe and by its little secrets.

One such secret was, for example, our habit of ringing the doorbell twice when we visited Oma's apartment, which was our secret code that it was us and not the *ganovim* (thieves). Or there was "Danny Kaye," a waiter who reminded us of the American actor, and nobody in the world (including the waiter himself) knew this was his name.

Or there was this cookie we called *Darfish*, a name that nobody else knew. It was a dream cookie, simple but brilliant: on a platform of crispy dough lay whole hazelnuts that stuck to each other with sweet caramel. Both ends of the cookie were dipped in chocolate. That's it. How did this cookie get its name? One day, my grandmother invited an acquaintance named Greta S. for coffee. Greta was a strict woman whose hair was meticulously chopped and almost shaved in the back. We all sat around the table on the balcony of Oma's small apartment in Tel Aviv, surrounded by cacti that were placed on the balcony's railing, collecting dust and bus soot. On the table, like a military parade ground, everything was ready for the *Kaffee und Kuchen* (coffee and cake) ritual: proud coffee cups, their handles to the right, armed with polished spoons, and some of those hazelnut cookies positioned on a serving tray. In front of them, like two plump First Sergeants—a sugar bowl and the creamer. And in the center, like a flagpole that everyone salutes—a pitcher with coffee! Lucie started pouring the coffee and asked everyone to get started, and my sister, Eva, reached for the serving tray and took a cookie. Greta's face got serious, and she commented that children should not take cookies without first asking "*Darf ich?*" (May I?). Lucie, Tante Liese, and my mother exchanged glances and said nothing, but after Greta left, they spent the rest of the afternoon and the evening in a ping-pong of resentment about the guest's nerve: "Who is she to teach us manners?" They said the words *Darf ich?* so many times that the next time they served this cookie, they called it *Darfish*, and the name stuck and was added to the secret language of our clan.

How we loved to say *Darfish* or "the short table" or "the green closet" (even though it was painted gray, but its name stuck)! Or to ring the doorbell twice, or to talk about Danny Kaye. When Greta

S. came for coffee again a few months later, my mom reminded us not to call the cookie *Darfish* in Greta's presence. Nor were we allowed to make the joke we'd invented: *Darf ich Darfish Kuchen haben?* (May I have *Darfish* cake?) These were our little secrets.

The big secret—the secret of my grandfather Hugo's death—was never discussed.

* * *

The box with the letters stood in my house in Menlo Park for at least a decade, waiting, and then, one day, I just had to know what was in the letters. I found a native speaker of German, a young woman named Nadine, who agreed to read and translate them to me. As we started reading, it became clear that these were letters from aging parents to a worried daughter in which many things were covered up. I learned a great deal, but when we were done, I had more questions than answers. Why did my grandparents go on this trip? Were they considering moving back to Germany, the country that had kicked them out just two decades earlier? The country that had killed millions of their people? What did really happen to them in Germany? And the biggest question: Why did Hugo want to die?

* * *

Meaningful conversations in my life tend to happen while I'm driving (I proposed to my wife at a stop light), and this is also how I had found out about Opa's suicide. It happened one day, somewhere at the end of the 80s, about 15 years before Nadine read me the letters. At the time, I lived with my wife and kids near Berkeley, and I was driving our old brown Volvo station wagon on the I-80 from San Francisco to Berkeley. I still remember the stretch of the highway where it happened and the loud roar of the station wagon. My mother, visiting from Israel, sat next to me. We were talking calmly, the way people talk at the end of the day after a good visit to the city. Maybe we had visited the museum or Chinatown. I don't remember. Somehow we started talking about health and from there, hereditary diseases. It occurred to me that I didn't know how Hugo, my mom's dad, had died.

"Actually, how did Opa die?" I asked my mom.

"He committed suicide. Didn't you know?" she shot back, gently brushing off responsibility for my ignorance.

"What?"

"This is not for the car," my mom ended the discussion, and her words kept pounding in my head all the way home. I didn't know. I knew that he died in his mid-60s, which back then was a reasonable age to die of a natural cause.

At dinner time that evening, my mother focused extra hard on her grandchildren, but once they were in bed, she knew that it was time to talk. We sat by the kitchen table, and she told me that five months after my grandparents had returned from their trip to Germany, her father jumped from the third floor to the bottom of the stairwell in a building in Tel Aviv.

She wasn't emotional. The only time my mother would cry was when she was caught off guard, and that evening, she had the whole dinner to put up her shields. I don't remember how I reacted. Hugging wasn't in our vocabulary. That evening, I didn't think of the horror joke I had told her as a teenager. That connection came to my mind years after she had died, and when it did, I closed my eyes and lowered my head and kept it down for a long time. How I wished that she could be there.

* * *

There was no shortage of one thing in my grandparents' letters from Germany: details. Hotel names, streets, and parks they visited, arrival and departure times of airplanes and trains—a favorite topic of my grandfather. And one day, a thought came to my mind: If the letters themselves could not shed light on Hugo's action, what if I could follow their footsteps? Maybe if I could ride the same trains, sleep in the same rooms, and sit in the same cafés as they had, I could get a better idea of why one person chose to live, and another one chose to die.

3 LOS ANGELES

"SHE'S ALWAYS REGRETTED HAVING GONE BACK."

Martin Mendel opens the door of his house in the Laurel Canyon neighborhood. He's close to 80 and reminds me of pictures of the two Mendel brothers, Hugo and Ernst, only I can't imagine either of them in a T-shirt. Martin's father, Ernst, who was my grandfather Hugo's brother, stayed in Germany after his brother, Hugo, left for Tel Aviv. Only in 1938, after the window of their shop was shattered on *Kristallnacht,*[1] did they flee the country to the Netherlands and from there to the United States. Martin is shorter than I am, a bit jumpy in his walk. We hug, and I feel his big hard stomach and that his hands are a bit frailer than before.

Martin has already told me on the phone that he doesn't know anything about my grandparents' 1956 trip. He was a young man back then, living in Los Angeles, while my grandparents lived in Tel Aviv. I told him that still, before I start following my grandparents' footsteps in Germany, I wanted to talk to people who had known them, and there aren't too many of those left. He said he didn't know them that well. For him, they were Uncle Hugo and Aunt Lucie who had left Germany for Tel Aviv in 1933 when he, Martin, was eight years old.

"They didn't go through the shit we did," he said, "But sure, I always love to see you."

Martin's house is packed with art he's carefully collected, and I like his taste. Yet in the past few years, after retiring from his job as a clinical psychologist, Martin began taking evening classes in painting and sculpture, and his works of art clutter the house. The statues he makes are impressive—a woman carrying a jug, two men wrestling in the nude—but his oil paintings are not as impressive, and they're all over the house. They are framed haphazardly, and he hangs them randomly wherever he finds a spot. So right next to a fine Japanese silk print of cranes hovering over a lake hangs a portrait of some model who was brought to the painting class dressed as a chef, and next to an old engraving of landscape in Europe hangs an amateurish picture of a guitarist.

In the kitchen, Martin makes me a sandwich. He spreads some mayo on the bread he got from Trader Joe's—the one with raisins he knows I like. His strong fingers grab some turkey cuts he got from the Armenian down on Laurel Canyon. A small piece of turkey gets stuck to the blue stone on his pinky, but he doesn't notice. Every few minutes, he clears his throat, producing a sound that's something between a cough and a shout. Some sort of music —classical or opera or a musical—is always playing in the background in his house, and from time to time he joins in. I learned not to get startled by a loud "Maria, I've just met a girl named Maria!" in the middle of our conversation. He turns off the music only when the TV is on, and after we eat our sandwiches, he puts on CNN, which we watch for a while. When they show George W. Bush landing a jet on the deck of an aircraft carrier and thanking the troops for their victory in Iraq, which has been shown *ad nauseam* during the past week, Martin turns off the TV with a big sigh.

"I haven't seen Eddie for a few days," Martin says, and he sounds a bit irritated by Eddie's disloyalty and a little worried. Eddie apparently is a blue jay who visits him often. Very often. Certain things never change on my visits to Martin's: the background music, the subtle hints about the infrequency of my visits, the bonding over George W. Bush, whom we both dislike.

I brought a pile of pictures with me, hoping that Martin would help me identify some people I don't recognize. Over banana bread and coffee, he sorts through them. With some he announces the identity of the subject flatly: "This is Onkel Max," (Uncle Max) or "this is our house in Menden," and I write it on the back of each picture. With other pictures, he thunders, "I think these are *goyim*. Not our kind." Or "I don't know who that is. She's too ugly to be related."

After a while, he gets bored, and I sense that he's making stuff up.

"Why don't you write on there?" he scolds me when he notices that I've stopped recording names on the back of the pictures.

I tell him that I'll only record names I'm 100 percent sure about.

"Who's going to argue with you now?" he asks.

* * *

He picks up another picture and bursts into laughter.

"Oh my God! Mary Fürstenberg..." He imitates a high-class petite woman with a squeaky voice who would come from Berlin wobbling on her high heels to visit her family in little provincial Menden wearing a chic hat and a fashionable coat.

Wait, that name sounds familiar. Oma and Opa mention in their letters some Fürstenbergs they'd met in Frankfurt. Are these the same people? "Sure," Martin says.

Mary Fürstenberg was a distant cousin. Her husband was an executive in the film industry in Berlin, and they managed to escape at the last moment, just before the war broke out, all the way to the Philippines. For a while, the choice that they made didn't seem too bad, but when the Japanese captured Manila, the

Fürstenbergs went through hell. One way or another they survived, and not long after the war, the Fürstenbergs moved back to Germany and settled in Frankfurt.[2]

* * *

He picks up a picture of his parents. Martin has a special way of holding things. He clutches onto things—a piece of paper, a picture, a slice of bread—as if his life depends on it. He grips the picture between his finger and his palm and looks at it for a long time without a word.

"It wasn't good for any of those people to go back to Germany," he says after a while. His voice is now soft and thoughtful, like the voice of an experienced psychologist, which he is. He tells me how his mother too went back to visit Germany.

For a long time, Else Mendel had resisted the idea. She had been in Los Angeles since 1940, worked hard, and became an American, as much as an immigrant can. As opposed to Oma who lived in Tel Aviv for 50 years without speaking any Hebrew, Else spoke fluent English. She even taught English to some Japanese immigrants, and Martin says that to this day, you can find whole Japanese clans in Los Angeles who speak English with a German accent.

People told Else that it was a good idea to visit Germany and heal the wounds, but she had refused. She couldn't forget the torch parades and shouting at night under their window, calling for the extermination of the Jews. Or the Nazi who'd forced her to kneel on her knees and sweep the glass of the showcase window that his buddies had broken the night before. Or how she had barely recognized her husband, Ernst, who had suddenly showed up one night back from the concentration camp—an emaciated man in a crumpled suit, blue marks around his neck, his head shaven, and a large bandage on his hand.

But people insisted that it was a good idea to visit Germany, and finally, Else caved, and one day in the 1970s, she flew to Menden, the little town in Germany where she, like my grandfather Hugo and his brother, Ernst, had grown up.

"I guess her fantasy was that once she got there, they will all come crawling and say how sorry they were about everything," Martin says and collects some crumbs of bread from the table. "Well, guess what: it didn't happen. She saw just very few people, and they were standoffish. They had to deal with their own guilt feelings, I guess."

At night, when she sat in her room, a stranger in her birthplace, there was no torch parade or shouting under her window, but there wasn't anything else either. Just an indifferent town that goes on as if nothing had ever happened. Else came back just a few weeks later and continued her life in Los Angeles.

"She always regretted having gone back."

* * *

I try to get something out of Martin about my grandparents' trip from Tel Aviv to Germany, but he really doesn't know anything about it, and it also seems true that he didn't really know them too well. Still, as he tells me about his father, Ernst, he compares him to his brother, and so I gather crumbs about Hugo. Martin seems right that "they didn't go through the shit we did." He knows that Hugo was also arrested by the Gestapo in 1933, but his detention was very short, and Hugo was not taken to a concentration camp like Ernst, who was released only after many weeks with the help of some connections with a police officer who knew the family. Ernst was an athlete, a muscle man. Hugo was a man of words. Ernst was an optimist. Hugo was bitter. This is how our brains work —comparisons. Else studied English in Los Angeles versus Lucie who did not learn Hebrew in Tel Aviv. Else played piano. Lucie didn't. And suddenly, something in common: Martin reminds me of something I had known but forgot: Hugo and Ernst's mother died when they were children, and they moved to their grandmother's house with their little sister, Liese. Martin says that their shared experience brought Ernst and Hugo close to each other.[3]

* * *

Before lunch, I'm in the other room when I hear a loud scream of a bird inside the house, and Martin's thundering voice:

"Eddie, where have you been?"

I inch toward the dining room quietly to avoid startling the bird. The patio door is open, and on the back of a wooden chair, under the painting of the chef, I see a large blue jay. Martin keeps demanding an explanation from the bird while his fingers dig into the loaf of banana bread. Eddie screams at the top of his lungs, maybe trying to explain his absence. Or maybe he's telling Martin that it's none of his business.

"And where's the madam?" Martin demands, and Eddie replies. Blue jays can be loud. Eddie seems to have exceptionally strong lungs, and his cries are amplified inside the house. Martin lays a chunk of banana bread on the palm of his hand. Eddie snatches it and flies outside and lands on top of the garage.

"It's our ritual," Martin says, grabs some more banana bread, and rushes outside. He throws pieces on the garage's roof while instructing Eddie where to get them.

"Over there, Eddie! Over there!" and Eddie follows his instructions, not missing a crumb. I don't know who enjoys himself more, Eddie or Martin.

4 NEW YORK

"SOMETIMES I HAD TO BEND."

"You're from Chicago?" the lady holding on to a walker at the end of the corridor asks me as I get out of the elevator. When I get closer, she gives me a welcoming smile. Gertrud Katz thinks that I'm someone else, from her side of the family, but I'm from her husband's side—Arthur—who was a cousin of my grandfather Hugo. Arthur had died decades ago, and Gertrud lives in the same apartment on Cabrini Boulevard in Washington Heights, New York, where they arrived in the late 1950s from Tel Aviv. She has short grey hair (its top insists on staying dark and young) and a thin face with bags under her eyes.

I explain to Gertrud that I'm the grandson of Hugo and Lucie Mendel and that I'm writing about a trip they took to Germany in the 1950s. Yes, sure, she remembers Lucie and Hugo, but she doesn't remember them going to Germany. She apologizes that she's 90 years old and that her memory sometimes fails her.

There are three walkers in the small apartment. A young Black woman named Julie helps out. Up until March 15, which was her 90th birthday, Gertrud used to take one of the walkers, the one with the wheels, get on the bus to Midtown Manhattan and walk around. But no more. We sit by a small table in the kitchen—

Gertrud, Julie, and I—and eat lunch, some cold cuts, tomatoes, bread, and potato salad that Gertrud made. Julie laughs when I ask her why she doesn't eat the potato salad. She's from Africa, she explains, and there you don't make a salad out of potatoes.

According to my calculations, the last time I saw Gertrud was 45 years ago when I was a young kid, but somehow I feel at home here. She speaks to me in English at first and gradually switches to German, which has the soft sound of our mini-tribe's German and takes me back to the Tel Aviv of my childhood and to the bigger tribe we belonged to—the *Yekkes*—Jews of German-speaking origin. While the *Darfish* cookies or joking about the waiter "Danny Kaye" were our unique family rituals, our culture was deeply rooted in that of the *Yekkes*: The *Kaffee und Kuchen* (coffee and cake) ritual or the *Schlafstunde* (their sacred siesta), and of course, their obsessive punctuality and attention to accuracy and details.

Some *Yekkes* integrated well in Israel, learned Hebrew, and started successful businesses or thriving farms. Others did not, and at least part of the reason often related to their difficulty with the local language. I ask Gertrud if she spoke Hebrew when they lived in Israel.

"I tried," she says and laughs.

My grandparents tried to learn Hebrew too, with very limited success. When they arrived at the port of Haifa in 1933, they were greeted by a cousin from Germany who had been in the country for seven years and spoke fluent Hebrew.

"In seven years, my Hebrew will be at least as good," my grandmother Lucie said (in German) and thus coined one of our favorite family sayings that she'd hear any time she would try to say something in Hebrew for the next 50 years. Something in the structure of this strange Semitic language was never welcomed in Lucie's and Hugo's European brains. So my mother (who was fluent in German, Hebrew, and English) served as a broker between her parents and the authorities. Her services as a translator were less needed on the street because many shopkeepers in Tel Aviv back then spoke Yiddish, which is related to German. So Lucie and Hugo (like many of their fellow *Yekkes*) spoke German to people who would then respond in Yiddish. They managed.

Gertrud's apartment is very clean, and it reminds me of Oma's apartment in Tel Aviv, which, come to think about it, had once been Oma's and Opa's apartment—Lucie's and Hugo's. But because of Opa's total absence, the apartment is registered in my mind only as Oma's place. I'm surprised that I understand almost everything Gertrud says in German, especially when she talks about simple things. She also switches to German when talking to Julie, and although Julie doesn't seem to speak German, she understands Gertrud's intentions. It seems that words are no longer needed for their routines.

From time to time, Gertrud forgets what she has already told me, but all in all, she is clear. And even when she gets confused a bit (something I had never experienced with my mother who died when she was 70), being with Gertrud feels cozily familiar. A few years after my mom died, one of her friends told me that she missed her so much that she found herself "chasing old *Yekke* ladies," and maybe this is why I chase Gertrud Katz.

For a while, Gertrud remembers, Arthur worked at my grandfather Hugo's factory in Bnei Brak near Tel Aviv. Riding on a bus was dangerous back in 1936 because the Arabs would shoot at passing vehicles. So when the bus would pass by the orange groves between Tel Aviv and Bnei Brak, the passengers had to lie on the floor. I ask Gertrud if she remembers Café Mendel that Lucie and Tante Liese opened on Ben Yehuda Street in Tel Aviv, and she remembers it very well and tells me how Lucie helped her find a job at another café on Ben Yehuda (that had so many *Yekkes* it was known as Ben Yehuda *Straße*).

Julie serves vanilla ice cream, and Gertrud tells me how later she and Arthur opened a shoe store on Dizengoff Street and how after Hugo lost his factory and all his money, he would stop by their store every morning to read the German newspaper, which was published in Tel Aviv for all the *Yekkes*—or at least for those *Yekkes*, like Hugo, who couldn't read Hebrew. On Fridays, Hugo would bring *Shabbos bonbons* (Shabbat candy) for Yael, Gertrud, and Arthur's daughter. But when I ask her to tell me some more about his visits to the shoe store, Gertrud's face suddenly darkens, as if she just this moment remembered how the story ended.

"Ach, Hugo, it was horrible when he threw himself from that building on Allenby Street. It was terrible." When I ask her for more details, she doesn't remember.

I show Gertrud a picture of Lucie, Hugo, and my mother, Mirjam.

"Is Mirjam still alive?" she asks.

"No, she died in 1992," I tell her.

"She died young then," Gertrud says. "I still remember how her husband died, and the child was just three months old. That was heartbreaking."

"That was me," I tell Gertrud, but somehow the comment doesn't register with her, and the *Yekke* in me is upset that not only did she forget that it was me, she doesn't get the facts right: I was eight months old when my father died—not three months.

"That was me," I repeat, but Gertrud looks into space.

"He was a nice man, that Rosen," she says. Julie asks if I'd like coffee, and Gertrud looks at the picture.

"Your last name is Rosen," she says after a while, "you were the little baby!"

"Yes, I was eight months old," I say.

"Sometimes one loses the string," she apologizes.

* * *

"That was heartbreaking," Gertrud said, but I don't remember my mom as a heartbroken person. She wasn't cheerful either. My father's sudden death made her cautious of surprises, and perhaps this is why she preferred the pre-packed one-liners that allowed her to navigate the world without showing too much of her real emotions. When you're by yourself, you can't expect too many surprises, and maybe this is why she was happiest when she would curl up in bed with a good book. (If we mocked her for talking to herself, she would shoot back: "I deserve to talk with an intelligent person once in a while.") Not that she was a loner. She loved people and had good friends, but her phrase "If anyone calls, tell them I died," fit her general desire to be left alone. (Although she used this particular demand for total isolation from the human race only before her sacred nap time—the *Schlafstunde*.)

My mom never felt sorry for herself, and my sister and I followed her lead. We were like all the other kids in our neighborhood, just with no dad. She also taught us tricks for self-sufficiency and survival, such as scratching our back against the doorframe if it was itching "the way pigs do," looking at our fingernails if we had the giggles during class, or biting our pinky if we felt that we were about to cry. I saw her do this a few times.

On Saturday mornings, she would play Brahms, Schubert, or Mozart on the record player that stood behind her bed, and she would dust her books or organize the house, and sometimes she would play the music we liked—*West Side Story* or *My Fair Lady*—and we would listen to her singing "Maria" and even try to join in with our broken English. And if I passed by her, she would look at me with her kind eyes and caress my cheek with the back of her hand. (This is also how she taught me to check whether an iron was hot enough—always with the back of my hand, never with my palm. Always ready to escape and contract.)

"Lucie was a wonderful person. She didn't have it easy with Hugo," Gertrud says. When she mentions Hugo's suicide again, she uses the word *Dummheit* (stupidity) to describe it.

"Dummheit?" I ask.

"Yes, it was stupid. He was a big lawyer in Germany, and he was no longer *Doctor* Mendel in Israel. He simply couldn't deal with it."

Before I leave, Gertrud cites a poem that was embroidered and framed on the wall at a family friends' home back in the German village where she had grown up:

> *Ich habe mir vorgenommen,*
> *klar durch die Welt zu kommen,*
> *es wollt' nicht immer glücken.*
> *Ich musst' mich manchmal bücken.*

(Free translation: I made a plan regarding the way I would pass through the world. I wasn't always lucky. Sometimes I had to bend.)

"And this is so true," Gertrud says.

I think about older people who may mix up details but keep a succinct summary in their mind of people from their past: "He was a big lawyer in Germany, and he was no longer *Doctor* Mendel in Israel." Sometimes one has to bend.[1]

5 ABOVE THE OCEAN
"NOTHING."

It's been six hours since we'd taken off from New York to Tel Aviv, and for the past 15 minutes, I've been staring at the digital screen. A thin white line stretches over a blue ocean, and on it—a small plane, like the guy who crossed Niagara Falls on a tightrope. But this guy just stands there refusing to move forward, as if he's considering turning around and going back to New York, but he doesn't want that either. What am I looking for in Tel Aviv at the end of the line? On the side of the ocean I just left behind, nobody knows anything about my grandparents' trip. Martin knows nothing. Gertrud doesn't remember. And they don't know much more in Tel Aviv. Ruth, my mom's cousin, already told me she only remembers that they went on that trip, but nothing more. Raphi, my mom's brother, told me all he knows, which isn't much because he was abroad at the time. The only person who knew all about that trip was my mother, and she's no longer in Tel Aviv.

I remember a different flight in 1992 (about ten years ago) on this exact route from New York to Tel Aviv. Just a week earlier, I hugged my mom in the hallway of the Beilinson hospital near Tel Aviv because I had to go back to work in Berkeley. We knew she was supposed to be released from the hospital the following day, and we could pretend we'd see each other again, but we both knew it was the last time. She bit her pinky so as not to cry, and I kissed her and went down the stairs where I could no longer hold my tears. I remember the knot in my stomach in the cab to the airport and on the flight back to the United States. But we were both wrong: It wasn't the last time we'd see each other. After a few days, my mom was hospitalized again. I had to see her one more time, and I flew to Tel Aviv through New York on this flight. When I entered her room at the hospital, she said, "Manu, thanks for coming." After a few days, my mom lost her voice, and I brought her a notepad on which (one-sided) fragments of our conversations have been preserved.

"How long have I been here?"

"Since I don't remember how I got to intensive care, I imagine I was pushed under the door."

"Sorry that I'm boring."

"I can't talk! Enjoy!" And repeatedly: "Visits no," "No visits!!!!!", "*No visitors except my cousin Ruth.*" On the last page, she wrote one word, and each time she wrote it, her handwriting became more difficult to read. Perhaps it was a reply to our questions of whether she wants something: "Nothing," "Nothing," "Nothing."

"If anyone calls, tell them I died," she always said before her nap time, and in 1992, people called, and indeed we told them that she died. Cancer. Yes, it was short. Beilinson Hospital. Seventy. Thank you.

It's now been six and a half hours since takeoff, and it seems that the little plane on the screen has moved a quarter of an inch toward Tel Aviv.

6 TEL AVIV

"YOOOO-HOOOO!"

It's a spring day in Tel Aviv, and I am standing in front of their apartment building on Reines Street. Up there on the first floor, my grandparents, Dr. Hugo Mendel and Lucie Mendel, were preparing for their trip to Germany in August 1956. And this is where their trip ended (in October 1956), with a green bath sponge in the shape of an elephant. The building hasn't changed a bit: the large Ficus tree with twisted external roots in the front, the dried-out fountain (if it had better days, I'd never witnessed them,) a piece of hard dirt that was supposed to be the garden. Cars are honking on the street behind me, and there's a strong aroma of burnt coffee in the air.

I remember standing here with Tante Liese (my grandfather Hugo's sister) when I was four or five. We had just gotten back from a short stroll and wanted Oma to come downstairs and join us for lunch. Cell phones were yet to be invented, and the intercom system (made out of black Bakelite) never worked. On my dad's side of the family (the Polish side), we had a family whistle, but the *Yekkes* had a different system—yodeling. Tante Liese filled her lungs with air and announced:

"Yoo-hoo!"

A few heads turned around, but we didn't care. We focused on the empty balcony. When nothing happened, Tante Liese went to the next level:

"Yoooo-hoooo!"

Nothing.

She let a moment pass: "Yooooooooo-hooooooooo!"

And then Oma appeared on the balcony, like a queen. For a split second now, I again feel the joy of seeing her up there.

Now, I walk into the yard, and I face the 14 beaten up mailboxes that are covered with stickers for pizza delivery, exterminators, and plumbers who are available 24 hours a day. (When I was a kid, there were no such stickers). I've seen Oma open her mailbox so many times, but for the life of me, I can't decide which one it was. Was it the upper one on the right? Or the one just below it? Martin would say, "Say that it's the upper left one. Who's going to argue with you?" But something in me wants the truth. There is truth. Things either happened or did not happen.

I walk into the entrance hall. The walls are covered with the same yellow tile that was always there. Sliding down the heavy wooden handrail on my butt was strictly forbidden by the landlord, Mr. Harmelin, but when it was just the two of us—Oma and me—she would wink at me, and I would do it. Should I go upstairs now? I just need to knock on the door and ask the current tenants to see Oma's place, and maybe they'll let me in. It's just one flight of stairs, and up there, I see the doorbell we used to ring twice to tell her it's us and not the *ganovim* (thieves). I go up. My heart is beating fast. I manage to climb just four steps before I freeze. Everything happened on these stairs: They went down these stairs the day they left on the trip, and they climbed these stairs the day they returned. And on the last day of his life, Hugo went down these stairs to jump off other stairs.

I'm back on the street in front of the house. I don't have the courage to go up. It's simpler here. Besides, here I look like someone waiting for a cab, not like a thief looking for a door that was left unlocked or a weirdo frozen on the fourth step. Maybe it's better that way. If the people who live there now would have let me in, their new furniture would have erased the apartment I have had in my head: the balcony surrounded by cacti, the table of the *Kaffee und Kuchen* (coffee and cake) ritual, the heavy black furniture crammed here after they moved from the big apartment, and the secretary desk that smelled of dry wood and old paper. How proud I was the first time that Oma allowed me to open that secretary desk by myself! And how much I loved playing with my grandfather Hugo's folding camera that was always there! (Press the button and it would extend the shutter with a quiet swish.) And the dozens of green envelopes printed with the lawyer Hugo Mendel's law firm address in Germany were in that secretary desk too: "Dr. jur. Mendel | Rechtsanwalt u. Notar | Hamm (Westf.) | Große Weststraße 24 ¹ | Fernsprecher 967."[1]

As a child, I remember this apartment as a happy place, and I try to cling to the *Darfish* cookies and the rest of the charms of our little tribe. But I realize more and more that it wasn't such a happy place when Lucie and Hugo lived here. "Lucie was a wonderful person. She didn't have it easy with Hugo," Gertrud Katz told me in New York, and though I nudged her to tell me more about it, she did not elaborate. And it is clear to me that before their trip to Germany, the tension and anxiety here broke all records.

My uncle Raphi told me that in the months before the trip, Hugo closeted himself in the little apartment, sitting for hours in bed in his buttoned-up pajamas, and when he wasn't in bed, he walked around the small apartment like a gun with the safety off. Worrying before one's travels—known in German as *Reisefieber*—was an integral part of any trip in my family, but the tension before this particular trip went far beyond a regular *Reisefieber,* and Raphi remembered it as being on the verge of hysteria. Could they

25

manage with their budget? Where should they stay in Düsseldorf? How much would a taxi cost from the airport to the hotel? Logistical questions that replaced the real anxiety.

My grandfather Hugo was known for his rage attacks, and I imagine him bursting at her: "You're not taking this suitcase!" he shouts.

"But my clothing, and we'll buy presents for the kids..." Lucie tries to argue.

"How will we change trains on our way to Wiesbaden with such a huge suitcase?" Hugo's voice intensifies.

"We'll take a porter, or we'll give the conductor a mark or two," Lucie tries.

"How long will the train be at the station?" he grills her.

"I don't know," she answers humbly.

At times, the tension got to the point that the whole trip was actually canceled. But after every boiling point, things calmed down, and cancellations were canceled. And in fact, some hope perhaps started blooming in his heart that things could turn around. No! The last word in the battle for Dr. Hugo Mendel's honor has not yet been said. It's not impossible. He knows several Jewish lawyers who returned to Germany and worked there now. People just like him who now had a decent desk, a secretary, and stationery with their name on it. Did he not study law just like them? Are they better than him?

"You're at least as good as they are," Lucie tries to appease him, and with the confidence they built in themselves, Lucie and Hugo send some letters and postcards to Jewish acquaintances in Germany: "We're coming!"

Yet anxiety is like a monster you see in the trailers for horror movies. You step on the floor tile in one room to stop it from crawling into the house, and it will try to sneak in through the faucet in the bathroom. You block the faucet, and it will slide through a crack in the shutter in the kitchen. And the moment Hugo informed his fellow lawyers that he was coming, he might already have imagined his encounters with them and was anxious by the comparisons between his life and theirs.

I think that four people in particular were on his mind: Ernst Katzenstein, Hermann Kugelmann, Manfred Herzfeld, and Erich Samuelsdorff—four Jewish lawyers like him with similar stories to his, but with different endings.[2] After Hitler took power in 1933, they could no longer appear in court in Germany because they did not belong to the Aryan race, and they all found themselves in Palestine which, at the time, was under the British Mandate. To practice law in the new country, a foreign lawyer needed to pass a special examination to demonstrate his command of the British legal system, which was different from the German system. Two of these people, Ernst Katzenstein and Hermann Kugelmann, took the exam, passed it successfully, and practiced law in British Mandatory Palestine. They were now both dealing with restitution and reparation issues and were going back and forth between Israel and Germany. The other two—Manfred Herzfeld and Erich Samuelsdorff—did not take the exams and did other things in Palestine. Herzfeld (who was married to Lucie's cousin) worked as a cashier at an insurance company in Jerusalem. Erich Samuelsdorff, who like Hugo had been a lawyer in Hamm, moved to Tel Aviv after the Nazis took over and lost his money in a small business he'd started.

Both Manfred Herzfeld and Erich Samuelsdorff went back to Germany at some point, and each represents a different ending to the story. Herzfeld represents a happy ending (relatively speaking) because in the early 1950s, he returned to work in his old profession. Samuelsdorff, on the other hand, returned with the hope of reopening his law practice, but he died before he was able to do it.

My grandfather Hugo belonged to the second group. Like Herzfeld and Samuelsdorff, he too did not take the exam, and like Samuelsdorff, Hugo went into business and failed. He bought machinery to make wire fences and barbed wire, opened a factory near Tel Aviv, and when the business failed, he had to sell it at a great loss and then worked as a salesman for the brothers who had bought the business from him. Maybe the big question now was: Would Hugo end up like Samuelsdorff, or would he be able to turn things around like Manfred Herzfeld?[3]

There's no doubt in my mind that Hugo thought about these four people as he was preparing for the trip. In fact, he would end up meeting the three who were still alive. But I don't know for certain that this was the reason my grandparents went to Germany. I'm just guessing here. It's possible that the trip was my grandfather Hugo's idea so that he could become again what he always was deep inside: a German lawyer. But maybe this whole trip was my grandmother Lucie's idea; perhaps she simply wanted to take Hugo to the last place where she had seen him happy—the region of Westphalia, Germany.

In the letters that they sent from the trip, they said they went to Germany to rest after 23 years in Tel Aviv. Maybe they even believed this, but to me, it sounds like a strange explanation. Quite a few German Jews were wandering in their homeland after the war, digging in the ashes. You can call this a lot of things, but "to rest"?

Whatever made them go and whoever had the idea, I know that in May 1956, two Israeli passports were issued for them and stamped with a permit that allowed them to leave the state of Israel to visit all other countries except for Germany. Israel did not have diplomatic relations with Germany, and this was the standard stamp, but then, the clerk who'd signed the permit at the office of the interior, drew a line through the words "except for Germany" and put his initials by the line that revoked the restriction. This procedure perhaps says it all about that period of bans and vows that started to be undone, about the Jewish state that was twisting and twirling between a vow to never forget and a monetary temptation that was becoming hard to resist.

In 1952, four years before my grandparents' trip, Israel and Germany signed a reparations agreement that was still generating a fierce debate in Israel when they traveled. Menachem Begin (later, Israel's prime minister), who represented the extreme opposition to this agreement, lived less than a mile away from their apartment in Tel Aviv. He vehemently opposed accepting money from Germany, arguing that this would exonerate it from its Nazi past, and as he spoke out against the agreement in the Israeli Knesset, thousands of his supporters surrounded the building, throwing rocks and stones. In contrast, Ernst Katzenstein (whom Hugo and Lucie planned to meet on their trip) was now at the center of negotiations with Germany as director of the Jewish Claims Conference in Germany, which represented the world's Jews in their dealings with West Germany.

Hugo and Lucie were clearly on Ernst Katzenstein's side of the debate (also when it came to personal compensation). There were people such as Greta S. (my grandparents' acquaintance of the *Darfish* hazelnut cookie fame) who refused to take any money, and there were those, such as Lucie and Hugo, who were fine with it. In fact, my grandparents' trip became possible because a few months prior, my grandfather started getting a small monthly allowance for the loss of his profession. (This claim was handled by a German lawyer from Hamm by the name of Friedrich Kieserling). I'm sure Lucie and Hugo didn't tell anyone about the money from Germany. I doubt they told many neighbors about their upcoming trip, certainly not their neighbor who owned a newsstand and refused to sell any German magazines or hear anything about Germany. He agreed with Menachem Begin: This money was stained with blood, and he would not step foot on German soil.

Lucie and Hugo didn't argue with that neighbor or with anyone else. They were way too busy dealing with their own anxiety.

I walk away from the building toward Dizengoff Square. In the weeks before the trip, when he did go out, Hugo occasionally would get confused, so usually Lucie went with him. I can picture the two walking together: she in a flowery dress, and he, a couple of inches shorter, dressed in a suit and tie, and with his belly ahead of him, like the letter D in the Dr. that always appeared in front of his name.

7 TEL AVIV
"SO PEE ON A BROOMSTICK!"

I would play at their apartment for hours with my grandfather Hugo's folding camera—pretending to load it with film, or pressing the button that would extend the shutter with that familiar quiet swish. I don't remember ever asking for film or inquiring what happened to that Hugo or Opa who had once owned this camera. There was nothing I liked better than strolling along with Oma on the streets of Tel Aviv—a boy who insisted on having his hand in constant contact with the hedges and fences of the city, as if he were a streetcar connected to a gigantic power generating system, and a tall woman who stopped from time to time to tell him that these fences are *schmutzig* (dirty). I grew up in the suburbs, so Tel Aviv's city center was never boring to me, and the same went for Oma, who had the curiosity of a child about the city and was also a bit of an ambulance chaser. If a crowd gathered on a street corner, we were there, and if anyone (usually my mom) accused Oma of being nosy, she would say, "I'm not nosy. I'm thirsty for knowledge."

How Oma and I communicated with each other is still a bit of a mystery to me, as she didn't speak any Hebrew, and I didn't speak any German. Or maybe that's not completely true. Once, when I was five, I had a sleepover at Oma's place, and before going to sleep,

I asked her, in Hebrew, for a handkerchief. She didn't understand me, so I repeated the word in Hebrew again and again. Oma was trying to guess what I meant by bringing miscellaneous items into my bedroom, from toys to books to pillows. In my frustration, I suddenly heard myself scream the word in German: "*Taschentuch!*"

So it seems that I had a small German vocabulary, some of it hidden, and come to think of it, this was also true for her Hebrew vocabulary. She knew, for example, to yell "*Ta'ut!*" (wrong number) in Hebrew and hang up on people (almost) like a native Israeli. Let's just say that we both had very limited vocabularies with extremely little overlap. But even though we didn't understand the meaning of each word, we understood the intention, which was usually good. The one time I can recall when my intention wasn't good, I cursed her, and she started laughing because for *this* I chose the German expression *alte Schachtel* (old bag). The truth is we also spent long hours in the small apartment without a word—she read her journals, and I dug in a drawer of old wires and burnt fuses or played with Hugo's folding camera.

Like my mom, Oma walked around this planet with prepackaged one-liners, although many of them drew on her German upbringing and so were very unclear to me. If you were to offer Oma potatoes or French fries, she would say, "Potatoes belong in the cellar!" If I'd lift a pot's lid to see what was cooking, I would hear, "He who peeks into pots will not go to heaven." If I were restless and she couldn't calm me down, she'd finally snap, "So pee on a broomstick!" And when she would talk about Greta S., who knew the latest gossip about everybody in Tel Aviv, she would say, "I need to visit Greta to hear how I'm doing."

8 TEL AVIV

"ZUFRIEDEN"

Around Purim, there was the photo ritual. We would walk up the hill to the bus station of our neighborhood, and there my mother would light a cigarette, and we would wait for the bus on the bench under the asbestos canopy. From time to time, a car would pass by, followed by the silence that stays with those left at the station. When bus number 23 would arrive, we would board it in a leisurely way and go to Elite, the bustling transfer station. There, at Elite, my mother would hold me tight because the next bus was much more crowded, and when the conductor would close the doors, he'd almost cut people in half. I was sure that one day I would be left alone in Elite and that my mother and Eva would continue to Tel Aviv without me, or the other way around, or worst of all—that they would arrive in Tel Aviv with only half of me.

We would get off at Dizengoff Street, and when we were close enough to the house, my mother would give us a nod and smile, and my sister and I would run ahead, rush upstairs, and ring the doorbell twice. For a few moments that seemed like eternity, we would stare at the door and then debate whether we should press the doorbell again, and after a few more seconds of excited anticipation, we'd hear the locks being opened, and we would see Oma and the light in her eyes.

Oma would help us with our costumes. My mother saw this as a nuisance, but Oma was completely into it and would plan the costumes for weeks. Then we would go to Photo Gilai and have our pictures taken. In 1956, my sister was "queen of spring," and I was a cowboy.

When Oma and I would walk together, I loved to hear her praise me when we would meet one of her *Yekke* lady friends on the street. Oma loved a good joke, and she used to tell her acquaintances all my clever remarks, which, I'm not sure she realized, often originated from a distorted perception of reality and not from a great sense of humor (when we learned about Passover in kindergarten, I asked her if she knew Pharaoh personally).

When her acquaintance would get out of earshot, Oma would sum her up to me with a short sentence. She classified many of them under the label of "*Hat viel mitgemacht,*" which meant she had gone through a lot. (The context was very vague to me. At the time, there was almost no discussion of the Holocaust, certainly not with children). About some of them, she would say, "*Es geht ihr gut,*" which meant that she was doing well financially. But the most important label, and one that she attached to almost every Frau we met (even to those who she had adorned with one of the previous labels), was that she was now *zufrieden*—content. *Zufrieden* was one of the most important words in Oma's dictionary, perhaps even more important than the word *schmutzig*, and I had the impression that Oma was the most *zufrieden* person in the world.

One time I was at Oma's place and the doorbell rang once, which meant that it wasn't us. She looked through the peephole and opened the door. An unshaved older man stood there holding an open suitcase with combs and shoelaces. He spoke Yiddish, and there was great sadness in the air, and Oma looked through his stuff and ended up buying a comb. It wasn't his last visit (and maybe not his first), and one time, Oma didn't want to buy from him any longer, and the man stood there and rang the doorbell once and twice and did not stop ringing.

9 TEL AVIV
"WHEN I GET TO BE THAT AGE, JUST SHOOT ME."

It was only when I reached my teens that I started to see that behind the jovial mask, there was another Lucie who was reflected in her daily phone call with my mom. Every evening between 7 and 7:30, the phone in the "hall" at our house would ring. Usually, even before the first ring was over, my mother was already by the kitchen counter, grabbing her Time cigarettes and a box of matches. The house was small, and my mother was thin and fast. At the second ring, she would once again pass through the "hall" and shout into space in German *Ich komme* (I'm coming). Now, a bit agitated, she would turn to the living room and ask herself, us, and the universe: "Where on earth did I put that ashtray?" On the fourth ring, she'd fall into the blue armchair and raise the handset at the same time, and then, without any introductions like "hello" or "good evening," she'd utter something prosaic in German such as: "Frau Pollack has just left," or "I've already spent 45 minutes with Tante Liese on the phone," thus continuing a conversation with her mother that's been going on for years and was interrupted occasionally by trivial things like work, food, and sleep. And so, every evening, for an hour or more, my mother would sit in the blue armchair, a burning cigarette in her hand, hosting a daily talk show in which the only listener was also caller number one who would bombard her with complaints about the cleanliness of Tel Aviv, questions about the operation of small household appliances, reports on health issues, the economy, and the state of the postal services around the globe.

The last topic would get daily coverage. There are worriers in every family, but my grandmother Lucie was a worrier of the first order. A family member who would travel abroad back then would not call (calls were complex and prohibitively expensive) but send a sequence of life signals in the shape of letters and postcards. For Lucie, two weeks without a letter or a postcard was a red flag. Three weeks without any sign of life was a desperate SOS. A month without a letter meant that the worst had already happened and that the telegram confirming it was already on its way—it would just be a matter of time before we got it.

Considering this side of Oma's personality, I can't think of a job less fitting than the one chosen by Raphi, my mom's brother. It turns out that in addition to his talent of wiggling his ears, he worked for the Mossad and spent most of his time abroad on secret missions. Thus every conversation with my mother would sooner or later include the sentence, *"Der Junge schreibt nicht,"* (the boy doesn't write). This was followed by a lecture by my mother about the work ethic of the Israeli letter carrier, a review of postal strikes in France (Paris was Raphi's base for many years), and—occasionally—a report of public services in the developing world.

But calming Oma down wasn't easy.

"How come Greta S. got a postcard from Belgium?" she would ask.

"But *Mutti* (mom), Raphi is in Paris, and *that's* where the strike is, not in Belgium," my mother would say patiently.

"He can use diplomatic mail," Oma would argue.

"But *Mutti*, diplomatic mail is not intended for personal use!"

"So he can send a telegram," she would conclude.

"To announce that he is still alive?"

My mother was a patient person. Once, when Lucie complained that she couldn't fall asleep at night, my mother advised her to count sheep. The following day, when Lucie reported that this didn't work, my mom pulled out the killer trick that worked beautifully for one of her friends—spelling long words in German starting from the end of the word. "You won't get past the letter 'W' in the word *langweilig* (boring)," she promised Oma. But my mom didn't take into account Lucie's inquisitive mind. The next morning, Oma called to say that she couldn't sleep all night. Something in this intellectual exercise woke her up in an irreversible way. My mother didn't give up, but sometimes even the most loyal personal assistant might show some signs of impatience—a raised eyebrow, a short sigh. And my sister and I saw the signs and heard the tone in her voice. ("*Mutti*, it hasn't changed from yesterday or the day before yesterday. The postal workers in Paris are on strike!")

One time, after an especially long talk show, my mother left less room for nuance. She put the handset down, exhaled the smoke from her lungs, sighed, and told my sister and me, "When I get to be that age, just shoot me."

10 TEL AVIV

"HOW COULD HE?"

Amid my research in Tel Aviv—of their preparation for the trip and Hugo's suicide after they'd returned—I meet my uncle Menda Rosen, my father's brother, who is about to move to a retirement home and gives me a folder he'd found while cleaning his shelves. It contains documents related to my father's death. I take it, but I'm not going to look at it. I'm focused on one death and don't want to deal with another.

Yet at night, my hands open the folder. There are letters of condolences and more letters of condolences. Letters of replies to letters of condolences and more of those. Obituaries, an invitation to the dedication of a street named after my father. My father was the financial adviser to the chief of staff in the young Israeli army. He was loved by many. I know all that.

One piece of paper catches my attention: an export packing list from the Underwood Corporation in Connecticut. After the death of my father, his two brothers purchased a typewriter for my mother so that she could supplement her income by typing after work. Now, 50 some years later, I picture the journey of one Underwood typewriter with a Hebrew orientation, from its loading on the ship Exilona in the New York Harbor to its arrival in early

October 1954 in Tel Aviv. I remember falling asleep to the staccato of this typewriter as my mom typed into the night: the cigarette, the coughing, the ratchety sound of the carriage return. And the ring at the end of each line.

And there's another folder, a much thinner folder, within that thick folder. When I open it, it takes me a moment to understand what I am looking at. It is a photographer's contact sheet with dozens of tiny little black and white pictures. Soldiers stand in line. Civilians are walking. Officers are carrying a coffin on their shoulders. I get a magnifying glass and look at the people walking behind the coffin. My God, it is my father's funeral. My heart is racing. Where is my mom? I can't find her. More pictures of officers carrying the coffin, young female soldiers are carrying flowers. Men in short-sleeved white shirts walking on the dirt road. I recognize Dr. Kanovitch, my pediatrician, walking with his bag. It's as if I am watching a black-and-white silent film of our darkest moment.

Suddenly I see my grandmother, not Oma, but my father's mother, Pnina. She is a short woman, exactly as I remember her, supported by her daughters, my aunts Channa and Chava. And then I see my mother in another picture—a scarf over her head, huge sunglasses —a 31-year-old who just a week ago was happy. I can't find Oma. Where is Oma? My sister was three years old, and I was a baby, so Oma must have stayed at home to take care of us. But next to my mother, I see him—Dr. Hugo Mendel.

He's wearing dark sunglasses and a white straw hat, one of the few men in a suit and a tie. I focus the magnifying glass on his face, and the only thought in my mind is "How could he?" This funeral took place in October 1953, and in March 1957, less than four years after his daughter was left a widow with two kids, Dr. Mendel jumped to his death. I can't think of him as "my grandfather" or as "Opa." I try to feel some compassion toward him, but all I feel is rage. I don't think I have realized up to this moment how angry I am at him for abandoning his daughter.[1]

11 MUNICH

"WE ATE STEAK WITH MUSHROOM SAUCE."

Did my grandparents hold hands when they took off from Tel Aviv? I tend to think that they did if for no other reason than this was the first flight of their lives. Planes were even noisier than they are today, so it's not hard for me to imagine that my grandmother Lucie gently put her hand on my grandfather Hugo's hand, maybe a little alarmed. True, they had been married for 35 years, and not all these years were good, but now, there was nothing my grandmother Lucie wanted more than to see Hugo *zufrieden*.

Shortly after takeoff, a passenger by the name of Lowenberg offered his seat to Lucie. He noticed that this was her first flight, and he wanted to give her a chance to look out the window. Lucie jumped at the opportunity, and as she was looking at the Mediterranean Sea below, she listened to the conversation that was unfolding between Hugo and Mr. Lowenberg. The guy already had a lot of credit with Lucie, as his gesture classified him as a *Kavalier* (gentleman), which was the biggest compliment a man could get from Lucie. And his credit went through the roof when it turned out that he was a judge in Tel Aviv, and a son of an old acquaintance of Hugo's from the Jewish student organization in Germany.[1]

Sitting next to a judge was a good way to start the trip, and sitting next to a judge who was a son of an acquaintance was even better. It brought back the days when my grandfather Hugo walked among lawyers, skipping the days he peddled wire fences from one hardware store to another. And a story about the generosity of a judge who was a son of an acquaintance was a good thing to report to my mom in their first letter, as they knew how worried she was and how much she hoped that this trip would start correcting the injustice done to her dad. And so the trip started on the right foot. They were surrounded by scents not common in ration-stricken Tel Aviv—the cologne of a flight attendant, the aroma of good coffee, the aftershave of a passenger. They sat next to people with good table manners who were talking in hushed voices. I found this Swissair postcard in Lucie's stuff from their return flight, and I'm sure they felt like the people in the picture also on their KLM flight from Tel Aviv to Munich. Here they are, Lucie, the judge, and Hugo, talking softly in German, as the plane glides over Athens, Belgrade, and the Austrian Alps and finally lands in Munich.

Because Germany had no embassy in Israel, Lucie and Hugo needed to continue all the way to Amsterdam to obtain German visas, and they spent their time in Munich in a closed area in the airport for a few hours before taking off. And this stop was also something of a test dive to make sure their diving suits could handle the pressure. Initially, I thought I'd include even this layover in my reincarnation of their trip. That I would eat a steak with mushroom sauce at the airport restaurant, as Hugo reported in his letter. But I decided to be a bit less pedantic and to skip Munich.

Still, I'm trying to guess what went through their minds there. One line of thought is not surprising: This was their first encounter with Germans after the war, and I'm sure they examined every policeman and waitress with the obvious questions: Was this guy a former SS officer? Had the lady behind the counter served as a guard in Dachau?

Yet deep in the immigrant's soul, you will often find a complication. How did they feel, for example, when they heard the first announcements in German? Maybe disgust and aversion, but possibly a familiar feeling of returning home. It had been more than 20 years since the last time they had been in a public place and understood exactly what was going on. In Palestine and Israel, they lived the lives of strangers who always needed translation or at least a clarification, and maybe now, for the first time, a new feeling of freedom went through their veins. Maybe here in Munich they started feeling the paradox that would be their companion throughout their trip: that they felt so much at home in the country that had rejected them. That they couldn't get enough of Germany, but that they exhaled with a sigh of relief when they took off for Amsterdam.

12 AMSTERDAM

"EVERYTHING WENT LIKE CLOCKWORK."

On the flight from Munich to Amsterdam, my grandfather Hugo looked out the window and tried to identify something familiar, especially when they were above Westphalia, the part of Germany where he grew up. His heart maybe quivered as you might expect from a person gliding over his childhood, but Hugo was reserved. "We didn't identify anything," he reported flatly in his letter to my mom. They would land in Amsterdam in the evening and in the morning, would go to the German embassy to get a visa. Hugo didn't report any worries, but given his last encounter with German officials, I'm sure he was anxious. And because I share his genes, I take the liberty of imagining the points he was rehearsing in his head during the flight for the argument he expected with those bureaucrats about why they *must* give him a visa. He was born in Germany, was he not? And wasn't that enough? And not to a family of some immigrants from the East, but to a family that had lived in Germany for generations (some say from the 17th century). He grew up and studied in Germany, served in the German army, earned a PhD from the University of Greifswald, and opened a law office.[1] So why exactly wouldn't they give him a visa? No, he had no intention of staying in Germany, if that's what the gentlemen were concerned about. And actually, what if he did? He had been born here! But no, he just wanted to see the country of his childhood one more time. Was that forbidden too?

A KLM minibus took them to the hotel. In the morning, they would go to get the visa, but for now, they could enjoy themselves and be "*vornehme Leute*" ("fancy people," another one of Lucie's favorite expressions). The way they described their suite at the Carlton Hotel, it sounded larger than the apartment in Tel Aviv that they had locked that morning. It included a bedroom, a living room, a small kitchen, a bathroom, "and all the luxury," as Hugo wrote. They never got used to the shouting on the streets of Tel Aviv, to people eating with their mouths open or holding the fork in their right hand. And in Amsterdam? European politeness. Nobody around them chewed with his or her mouth open. Everyone was holding the knife in the right hand and the fork in the left. Amsterdam was Europe without the emotional baggage, or at least with less baggage. My grandmother Lucie would remember Amsterdam as the most beautiful place of their whole trip, but it was impossible for Hugo not to think of his younger brother, Ernst, and his family, who had been refugees in this city before the war.

* * *

I'm eating breakfast at the Lloyd Hotel. (Why can't they make such good baked rolls in California?) Over its long history, this place served as a youth detention center, a migrants' boarding house, and as a space for artists. Recently, it has been converted into a hotel, and somehow, I find myself here and not where Hugo and Lucie stayed. After they managed to leave Germany, Ernst and Else Mendel were here for a few months with their kids, Martin and Judith, waiting for their visas to the United States. Martin told me that Wilhelmina, the Queen of the Netherlands, would pass in her car by the building, and wave at the refugees. When the Mendels' visas finally arrived, it turned out that their tickets for the ship that would leave from Hamburg could not be transferred to tickets from Amsterdam, and they didn't have money for new tickets.

I want to tell the waitress about this, and as I put down the cash, I say that my mom's cousin was held here before World War II.

"You wouldn't believe how many relatives of people who were held here visit this place," she says, as she takes the money. I want to tell her the rest of the story, but she's already taking the order at another table.

I wanted to tell her that after a few days of despair, they found an envelope in their room one evening with the money they needed. Martin told me that they never found out who'd left them the money, but he was pretty sure their Dutch relatives (from his mother's side) left it. "Have you ever asked them if they did it?" I asked Martin. "They were all murdered after the Germans invaded the Netherlands," he said.[2]

* * *

In the morning, Lucie and Hugo woke up early and went to the German embassy, and I imagine that the practice argument continued in Hugo's head. He was born in Germany. (Isn't that enough?) And come to think of it, his family may have lived in Germany from the 16th century, not the 17th. It's true that he didn't serve on the front during World War I, but he was guarding prisoners of war, and this was needed too, no? And had he mentioned to the gentlemen that his law office brought bread to the tables of a few German families?

Nobody argued with him at the German embassy. A bored clerk charged them 15 guilders and stamped their Israeli passports with a visa, and they found themselves on the street, maybe a bit surprised. "Everything went like clockwork," Hugo reported on the back of a postcard that featured the Rijksmuseum. At 1:45 they were, once again, on a KLM plane, this time on their way to Düsseldorf.

13 DÜSSELDORF

"THEY CAN ALL KISS MY ASS."

I get in a taxi at the airport and give the driver the name of the hotel, exactly as they did. Oblivious to his role in this historical reenactment, he pushes the meter button without a word, and the new Mercedes takes off quietly.

It's very green outside. They were here ten years after the war, and the greenery soaked everything with a sense of abundance and goodness. How different this must have seemed to them from the scorched Israeli summer they had left behind. A church steeple, street names with umlauts, a streetcar, men in suits crossing the street. They were not in Tel Aviv anymore.

Like an engineer who's here to study the site of a nuclear meltdown, I sit back into the soft leather seat and take notes. Something went wrong on this trip, and the first cracks showed up here in Düsseldorf. What happened to Hugo here? If you read their letters, nothing special. Writing to their daughter, Hugo and Lucie had one thing in mind: not to make her worry any more than she already was. But another paper trail that this trip left behind tells a different story.

* * *

"Shhhh…"

In the taxi, Ruth Shuttenberg, a friend who came to greet them at the airport with a bouquet of roses and teary eyes, kept shushing Lucie who couldn't stop gasping as she was looking out the window. Lucie would calm down for a while and then exclaim something again.

"Shhhh…"

The eyes of the driver perhaps appeared in the mirror, wondering about the people in his cab who sounded so German and yet were not. What about the lady holding a bunch of roses, pointing out the window? And the other woman hushing her? And why is the old man so quiet?

My cab stops with a screech in front of a small café on a busy street. It's a modest four-story building.

"Lindenhof Hotel?" I ask, and the driver points a few yards ahead to the hotel entrance between the café and a photo supply shop. My room at the hotel isn't ready, but they're just about to finish cleaning it, and the man at reception tells me that I can go up and leave my stuff there. Two maids with Middle Eastern complexions are making the bed and start laughing when they see me. It's more than a giggle. It's uncontrollable laughter as if I caught them in the middle of something forbidden. I leave my suitcase in the room and go downstairs to send an email home to let them know I have arrived safely, which is also the first thing that Lucie did after they'd arrived. Hugo preferred to stay in the room, and Lucie and Ruth went downstairs to send a telegram to my mother (which I also found in the box of letters): "Safely Arrived. Parents."

I go down to the street. The names of the streets that I recognize from their letters jump out at me. From Oststraße I turn to Graf-Adolf Strasse that Oma described as a fancy street (it's less so today). As I turn, I notice the main train station that I know so well from one of the postcards they'd sent. I spent a long time staring at that postcard through a magnifying glass, imagining the place. And suddenly it's here as if only now I realize that this isn't just a story. Everything actually happened. They were here.

Everywhere I go, I hear German. Not only around me but also in my head. It's completely insane: totally random words like *Obstsalat* (fruit salad), *selbstverständlich* (of course) and *unbestimmt* (no idea what that means) are heard in my head. Actually, most of the words are like *unbestimmt*—words that pop in mind with no meaning whatsoever. Those long walks with Oma in Tel Aviv left me with an impressive vocabulary of words I don't understand.

Back in the hotel, as I get out of the elevator on the second floor, I see a large red shopping bag filled with paper waste leaning against the wall next to my room with one word printed on it: Hugo. At night, I lie in bed on my back with my eyes open. The room is on the rear side of the hotel, and it is very quiet. I try to guess what Oma was thinking about when she was lying here in the dark. She probably was traveling in her map of pain. There was the pain of insult of Hamm, 70 miles east of here, the city that rejected them. There was the longing for Wiesbaden, in the south, where they spent their most precious time with little Mirjam. There was the searing pain of Northeim, farther east, the city where Lucie was born.

The longing. The feeling of guilt.

Northeim.

And Hugo? What was Hugo thinking about when he was lying here awake on his first night back in the old country? When my thoughts go there, I don't find anything beyond a few pieces of paper—a bunch of documents and letters—and I fall asleep.

The following afternoon, a little surprise was waiting for Hugo and Lucie in their room, a bowl of sugared forest berries that had become a distant dream in the past few years in Tel Aviv, where they had to stand in line at the grocery store for the family rationing of eggs and bread. It was their friend Ruth who had sent the treat to their room after they had mentioned in passing how much they missed those berries.

A bowl of sugared forest berries was a perfect thing to mention in a letter to my mom. See? You don't have to worry. We're pampered by friends, stay in luxury suites, the food is fantastic, and the portions are enormous. But my mom was worried. My dad's unexpected death three years earlier put her on edge, and her father's long spells in bed and his occasional memory lapses in Tel Aviv gave her reason to worry. How was he doing in the old country? Oma noted in a letter how well Hugo finds his way around. But she also said that sometimes, especially in the section around the train station that was heavily bombed during the war, he gets confused as he tries to figure out where a small street has gone. Is it him, or is it Düsseldorf? Is it his brain or this perforated city? Both here and there, segments were erased—detailed streets and alleys turned into wide boulevards. And how was her mom handling her pain? Would she go to Northeim, the epicenter of her agony?

After putting us to bed at night, I imagine my mom reading and rereading their letters, trying to figure out if they're hiding anything. She absently picks at the skin around her fingernails (that would always be red, sometimes bleeding). She lights a cigarette and inhales the smoke, and the rage about the injustice that was done to her father builds up inside her. But maybe there's hope? She tilts her head up a bit and exhales a long puff of smoke. Maybe he'll get a second chance? He already met a judge who's a son of a friend, and he surely will meet other lawyers. It sounds like her parents are having fun. I'm sure my mom wanted to buy into the sugared version that they meticulously try to build. Maybe she did. Their coverup was almost perfect.

While they painted a picture of a luxury vacation, Lucie pulled no punches when writing about the Germans, and this is how she summarized her first days in Düsseldorf: "They can all kiss my ass." She didn't write about the atrocities of the war. Reading her letters, you'd have the impression that what got her fuming was the prosperity all around her. It started in the taxi from the airport. Initially, when I read about Ruth shushing her in the cab, I thought that Lucie was shocked by the destruction she saw everywhere, but after more careful reading, it became clear that she was amazed by the fast recovery. By rows and rows of new houses. In the following days, she continued protesting: Israel was just starting to recover from a major recession,[1] and here, just a decade after the war, the Germans live in modern buildings, take fancy vacations, and go to Königsallee, the elegant shopping boulevard, to buy jewelry, china, leather jackets, and perfumes. "What's happening here at restaurants, cafés, porcelain, furniture, fashion, and lingerie shops is beyond words," she wrote. Her fury made her shoot in all directions. "Well, I told you enough for today," Lucie ended one of her letters. "I just forgot to say that the *Goyim* are disgusting. They all look alike, like blacks."

I have to say that it wasn't easy to read some of my grandmother's comments about other races. I tried to remind myself that she was born in the late 19th century and that I am reading her letters in the 21st century, but my discomfort didn't exactly fade away. Her sweeping generalizations about gentiles were a bit easier to digest, not because I share them but because I understood the emotional turmoil that she experienced, and I knew exactly where these comments were coming from—not from bitterness over jewelry, china, leather jackets, or perfumes, but from something so precious that she couldn't even discuss.

As opposed to Lucie, who wasn't shy about how she felt, Hugo was reserved and focused on logistics and listing cafés and restaurants where they dined. His underlying message was: All is under control, and we're spoiling ourselves. But in trying to maintain their coverup, Hugo and Lucie made one little mistake. Judge Lowenberg (who had given Lucie his seat on the flight) stayed at the same hotel, and when he was about to leave for Tel Aviv, they asked him to call their daughter to tell her that all was well. Lowenberg did, and I'm sure he intended to deliver the rosy news that they'd requested. My mom wasn't the type who would grill someone on the phone, but perhaps she detected hesitation in his voice, or maybe he blurted out the word "doctor," and she asked him a question that as a judge (and a *Yekke* judge at that), he could not lie about. Whatever happened, after my mom hung up, she sent them an express letter: "Are you telling me everything?" and Oma immediately dismissed her concerns in a return letter: "We are perfectly fine! Dad had a swollen cheek due to toothache," she wrote and added that now both his cheeks are swollen because the food is so good and the portions so large.

When I first read Oma's response, I even believed her, but in the coming months, I would find a report from Dr. Fritz Spanier, a physician from Düsseldorf who examined Hugo about 48 hours after their landing. He described a patient complaining about total exhaustion, spinning, and shortness of breath. Rereading their letters from that week, I found slight hints as to what was going on. Only now, Hugo wrote to my mom, he feels how tired he had become in the past 20 years. "I urgently need some respite," he wrote. And Oma wrote, almost begged, "He needs some rest!"

Something happened that led him to see Dr. Spanier. Perhaps Hugo collapsed on a street corner holding his chest; maybe he fainted in the hotel dining room. Maybe it was something else. Fifty years left enough dust to cover this.

* * *

I walk to Königsallee, which indeed is fancy, and from there to the Rhine through the old city. A brass band, all dressed in yellow, is playing a cheerful tune. I sit on a bench by the river and eat ice cream, the wind is warm, and everything is hazy. Nobody knows me here. If I die on this bench now, as Ernst Mendel did on a bench in Los Angeles, there will be 15 minutes of commotion, and the following day the ice cream guy will tell one of his regulars that yesterday a tourist died on a bench by the river. In May 1953, Ernst, Hugo's brother, walked in downtown Los Angeles, a 60-year-old immigrant with a leather briefcase. He sat down on a bench to rest.

After a while, people noticed that the man wasn't moving, and someone called an ambulance. Ernst died of a heart attack.

I continue along the river. A young Black man—his skin is the darkest I have ever seen—is rollerblading backward in an impossible slalom, finding his way through upside-down red cups that he had placed on the sidewalk. He's wearing a bright white shirt and a helmet that is half orange, half green. All eyes are on the guy—the Jesse Owens of rollerblading.

The director Fritz Lang, who immigrated to the United States because of Hitler and returned to Germany after he was placed on the Hollywood blacklist, once said this about the immigrant's destiny: "And when he returns, he is a stranger in his own land, and this I think is the real tragedy of immigration." Hugo was completely anonymous back in Germany, and it hurts to be nameless in a place that used to be home. It's like returning to a former workplace and realizing that although you were sure you couldn't be replaced, life does go on without you. The streetcars, the businessmen hurrying to their meetings, the bustling department stores—they all represented a painful truth: Germany managed very well without Dr. Hugo Mendel. Maybe he would have been less shocked if he had visited right after the war in 1945 to witness the destruction and the hunger. It's hard to know what he felt because he didn't express feelings in his letters, neither sorrow nor anger. Just once he commented in a letter to my mom, "The politeness is still here, but I find in me only bitterness." Except for this rare admission, he reported laconically, "Mirjam, we got your express letter." Or "We sat at Café Rütten," or "On Saturday, we visited the Loewensteins' charming new apartment, and we met a widow there of a judge I had known." As far as judge Lowenberg's phone call to her, he wrote, "There isn't and wasn't any reason to worry."

14 DÜSSELDORF
"TALKING NERVOUSLY ALL THE TIME – AND SAYING NOTHING!"

A postcard that Oma and Opa sent to me that week features a family of hedgehogs in worn and patched clothes. The parents are arm in arm: mother hedgehog has her hand gently on her daughter's shoulder. Father hedgehog has his hand on his son's shoulder. The caption under the picture reads, "We are happy." They are poor hedgehogs, but they are thankful for their good fortune, and they're looking forward. Only forward.

Lucie reported that they kept a low profile and spoke only with Israelis. Part of this came from her rage at all Germans, but there must have also been some fear. After all, there were enough people on the street who, just a decade ago, had been killing Jews full-time (or those who had not actively participated but thought it wasn't a bad idea). Lucie and Hugo also knew that not many Nazis had been punished severely and that many former Nazis were now holding senior positions in all areas of life. So beyond their role as shoppers, guests, and diners, they did not interact with non-Jews, which was certainly convenient for most Germans at the time. The war left destruction everywhere, and (despite Lucie's protest regarding the fast recovery) there was also poverty in Germany. And there were ruins, cracked walls, and rickety roofs. Germany was busy building its future and not unearthing its past.

Ten minutes from their hotel, one could find a classic example of just that. At the psychiatric clinic of the Medical Academy of the Rhine Hospital in Düsseldorf, planning was underway for new construction to reduce the severe overcrowding created by the bombing. During the war, several physicians at the hospital had been involved in the murder of mentally ill people under the guise of euthanasia as part of a Nazi plan to ensure the purity of the Aryan race. However, in a trial of these physicians in 1948, they were acquitted after claiming, in their defense, that they had not refused to participate in the process to prevent a worse situation, and in this way, they claimed, they had actually saved some patients. One of the acquitted, the psychiatrist Friedrich Panse, was now the director of the clinic. He devoted his energies and efforts to the design of new buildings, including a modern clinic, the first of its kind in Germany, for the intensive care of patients for short stays. Years later, some young German investigators would cry out as to the extent of Dr. Panse's involvement in the extermination of people with a mental health condition in other cities, but for now, it was easy to ignore.[1]

At the time, very few Germans (especially among those who suffered due to the Nazis) tried to talk about what had happened, and most Germans avoided the subject. "You can't imagine this complete silence," Mechtild Brand, who was born in Hamm during the war and started asking questions as a teenager, wrote to me.[2] Mechtild wrote a book about the Jews of Hamm, and over the years, I have been seeking her help in trying to learn about Germany. "People were hyperactive, talking nervously all the time – and saying nothing!" she added. When she asked the adults in Hamm about Jewish persecution, she faced a wall of silence. "In Hamm, I was told, 'There were no Jews, so there was no Jewish persecution!'" she reported to me.

Lucie and Hugo were invited to a few houses in Düsseldorf, all homes of Jewish families who at some point had spent time living in Tel Aviv (this is what she meant by "Israelis"). Coffee at the Loewensteins, lunch with the Pincoffs, lunch with the Benedicts. (Käthe Benedict, who was married to a Jew, was the only gentile Lucie liked. "She's not like the other *Goyim* with their short, red leaky nose," she fired off again in all directions.)

As far as the taboo on discussing the Holocaust, at least in their letters, Lucie and Hugo fit well into the general German atmosphere at the time. Not a single word. I have the feeling that they didn't discuss it with one another either, and that they were especially careful not to mention Northeim, the city Lucie was born in, and that if Northeim was mentioned, a long silence followed.

A thick blanket of silence covered everything, and if the past was hidden, how much more was the future? When Lucie wandered through the streets of Düsseldorf, she could not imagine how one day the energetic psychiatrist Friedrich Panse, director of the psychiatric clinic in Düsseldorf, would serve as an obstacle in the war for the honor of Dr. Hugo Mendel.

15 DÜSSELDORF

"OPA WAS A ZIONIST UNTIL HE GOT OFF THE SHIP IN HAIFA."

Why didn't they turn around? Dr. Spanier's report showed that Hugo was exhausted, and Lucie sounded bitter and resentful in her letters. So why didn't they get a flight back to Tel Aviv? Or barring that, why didn't they simply leave Düsseldorf? In the next couple of letters, they singled out Düsseldorf as the problem—a crazy and restless city—and they kept saying they wanted to leave for Wiesbaden where they had spent a vacation with little Mirjam back in 1925. They were longing for Wiesbaden as if they would find the young versions of themselves there, chasing their three-year-old daughter with a camera, laughing at her jokes. So why not move on? Something must have kept them in Düsseldorf.

The German words in my head settle down a bit after some time in Düsseldorf. I still hear random words such as *unglaublich* (incredible) or *Schönheit* (beauty). Sometimes I hear a fragment of a sentence in German inside my head, followed by another, as if Lucie and Hugo are arguing within me.

"Look how beautiful..." he says.

"I cannot enjoy this beauty," she says.

"Look how beautiful the river is," he says.

"We have rivers in Israel," she says.

"Rivers..." he scoffs.

As the days went by, Hugo stayed in their room for longer stretches, and Lucie walked the streets, looking, hating, arguing not only with him but also with herself. She craved the luxurious porcelain and fashion, but at the same time, it reminded her of everything that had been robbed from them. All those people walking around with fancy stuff could have been them—Lucie and Hugo—and as if she was shocked by the very thought, she immediately added, "No! I would not have wanted to be one of them!"

She was drawn to the beauty of Germany. Not to the buildings, which she called "an architectural chaos," but to nature: the Rhine River, the sky, the light, the wind in the trees in which yellow and orange spots now appeared. "I forgot how beautiful everything here is," Lucie wrote, and wished she could share this beauty with us. What she saw captivated her and hurt her at the same time. "I cannot enjoy this beauty," she wrote in one letter.

* * *

I'm in Menlo Park, looking through some boxes that I have brought from my mom's house. There are a bunch of old blue Israeli passports in one of the boxes: my mom's, Tante Liese's, Oma's, Opa's. And suddenly I notice two green passports, with a black eagle on each. German passports. I open one: Lucie Mendel. I open another: Hugo Mendel. My heart sinks. I'm the last person who's entitled to get upset at this because I've been living in California for more than 30 years with an American passport (and an Israeli one), but my heart doesn't listen. Under their pictures, a big stamp: "Düsseldorf 21. Aug. 1956." This is six days after they'd arrived. So these are the handcuffs that kept them in town. Mystery solved. When they arrived in Düsseldorf, they applied for German passports, and then, they stayed until the documents were ready. Growing up, I never knew that Oma had a German passport, probably because it was hidden deep in her closet. Most Israelis back then saw the act of getting a German passport as pure heresy. Why did they do it? To avoid the future need for a stopover in Amsterdam to get a visa? Or were they thinking of returning permanently to Germany? I don't know the answer, but I know that I'm holding two green passports for Hugo and Lucie Mendel. Nationality: German. Hugo's occupation is listed as a merchant, agent, and Dr. jurist (JD), squeezing in just one line everything that he was and is and maybe hoped to be again. Lucie's occupation is listed as housewife. She almost looks like she's biting her lips in the picture.

If I have to guess who pushed for this move, Lucie or Hugo, it's clear to me that it was Hugo, who had had bumpy relationships with Zionism. My mother used to say, "Opa was a Zionist until he got off the ship in Haifa." She mentioned a few times that he even attended one of the Zionist congresses, and growing up, I was sure that my grandfather Hugo Mendel was a significant figure in the German Zionist movement. But as I became interested in Hugo and leafed through books about the history of German Jews, I never found his name. In the index, just before the name "Mendelssohn, Moses," where the name Mendel would have appeared, there was always another name—Melamed, or Machovsky, but never "Mendel, Hugo." Only once did I come across Hugo, and not in the text, but a picture. I was browsing in a book about Zionism in Germany before 1933 when I suddenly saw my grandfather, at the lowest left corner with 15 Jewish students at the University of Bonn. Some of them had wide smiles on their faces. Some were more serious. Hugo had a tiny smile, and his lips were not yet drawn bitterly downward.[1]

Then came Hitler and the letter that prohibited Hugo from appearing in court, and Hugo's theoretical Zionism turned practical. They immigrated to Palestine where he opened the factory for mesh wire fences and barbed wire. Why did he decide to become an industrialist rather than trying to continue as an attorney? "The wisdom of the lawyer is the wisdom of the tongue," wrote Supreme Court Justice Haim Cohn (one of the *Yekkes* who integrated very well into the Israeli legal system). Hugo realized that he would need to learn Hebrew and English to work as a lawyer in Palestine, and maybe at the age of 42, he could no longer bear the thought of being scolded by young teachers who would correct his pronunciation and mistakes. As an industrialist, he would convert the small capital he saved into something tangible that everyone needed—fences. From his experience in law, he knew that there would always be a demand for boundaries.

Why did the business fail? Hugo's lack of experience in manufacturing and the fact that Palestine, as the rest of the world, was under a severe economic depression, didn't help. But there were other reasons: Language is important in business too, and despite some attempts to master it, Hugo spoke almost no Hebrew. Perhaps most important: his mentality didn't fit the way business was done in the new country. If a meeting was supposed to start at 9 a.m., he expected people to show up at 9 a.m. and not at 9:30. If an invoice was due by the end of the month, he could not comprehend why it wasn't paid even after two months. He didn't connect with Jews from Arab countries nor with the *Ostjuden*—the Jews from Eastern Europe. In 1939, he sold the business at a loss and became a salesman at the business he had started.

Back in Germany, some old-timer Jews whose families had been in the country for generations tended to look down on *Ostjuden*. The old timers read Goethe and Schiller, dressed like Europeans, had refined table manners, and spoke proper German (not Yiddish, which was seen as butchered German). When I visited Martin in Los Angeles, he read me a letter Hugo had written to his brother, Ernst, in 1939. By then, Hugo had been in Palestine six years, and his letter reeks of bitterness and pessimism: "It looks like the Jewish efforts here are winding down," he wrote in a doomsday note about the future of Jews in Palestine. True, the *Ostjuden* still said that everything would turn out to be all right. *"Es vet zein gut,"* Hugo mocked their Yiddish (Martin laughed like a kid when he read it to me), but they didn't base their belief on any economic or political knowledge, Hugo continued. All they cared about were deals.

And he was sickened by the constant violence too. In the same letter, Hugo told Ernst about a young Jewish woman, a radio announcer, who was killed when a bomb in the radio station had gone off. Hugo knew her parents, and he wasn't yet sure who was responsible for the terrorist attack, the Arabs or the Jews. "If it turns out that Jews did this attack, one can only feel disgusted," Hugo wrote.

Lucie went through an opposite process compared with Hugo's. In 1933, before they'd left Germany, Hugo had to persuade her to leave the deep green of Germany for dusty unfamiliar yellow. She must have been a bit shocked when they arrived. I found a picture from a trip they had made to the Dead Sea shortly after they'd arrived in Palestine. Lucie stands in the mud in a slim, fashionable dress and high heels, and her expression says, "What is this?" When he said "lake," she must have imagined swans and a green forest reflected in the water. What was this thing? Their first home in Tel Aviv was a spacious apartment on Chovevei Zion Street (the lovers of Zion), and I think that at first there was only one lover of Zion there named Hugo Mendel. But Tel Aviv has always been an interesting city, and Lucie's inquisitive eyes found endless scandals and amusing scenes there.

And most importantly—people! Lucie soon discovered that she was not the only German speaker in the city, and she picked up her *Yekke* friends. It seems that Hugo was less sociable by nature. And another thing: Hugo had no relatives in the new country (except for Arthur Katz, the owner of the shoe store), as opposed to Lucie, who was blessed with cousins. Her father had ten siblings, and some of the sons and daughters of these siblings now gathered in Palestine and became part of the Zionist enterprise. There was the one who raised cows, the one whose daughter was killed when the Italians bombed Tel Aviv in 1940, or the ones whose son was killed in the Convoy of 35 during Israel's war of Independence. As opposed to my grandfather Hugo, who was becoming increasingly withdrawn, these disasters, along with the reports that began to arrive about the fate of the Jews who'd stayed in Germany, seemed to have tied my grandmother Lucie to the new country. She certainly was worn out by two decades of hard work and economic stress in Israel, and she had a lot to say about the shouting on the bus, the rudeness at stores, and the *schmutzig* sidewalks, but she felt like an Israeli. And it seems that their trip to Germany brought out, even more, the Israeli in Lucie. When they were still waiting for their passports in Düsseldorf, Lucie went shopping one day when someone accidentally bumped into her and immediately apologized. Without thinking, Lucie responded in Hebrew: "*Ein Davar*" (never mind) and continued walking.

"And the idiot didn't even get what I said," she wrote to my mom. Her letters were now sprinkled with the few Hebrew words she knew. When she wrote about Israel, she used "we" or "us" as opposed to Hugo who used neutral terms such as Tel Aviv or Israel. When comparing German kids to "our kids" in Israel, Lucie was proud of how healthy and beautiful the Israeli kids were as opposed to German kids who looked hungry with adult faces. I wasn't surprised to see that she never renewed her German passport, which expired after five years.

A man, a woman. His passport, her passport.

I think he felt good about the passport that took him back in time, documenting his academic degree, his profession as a lawyer, and the fact that he'd been born in Germany. I think she would have been happy if her German passport got lost. How did their kids feel about their parents' German passports? My guess is that their kids were split on this as well.

Ludwig, my mom's brother, who became Raphi in Tel Aviv, was an enthusiastic Israeli. From his first day in Tel Aviv at the age of seven, he connected to the never-ending stream of adventures the city offered: walks to the beach, street fights, soccer games, and caravans of camels carrying wooden crates filled with sand from the beach to building sites. School was less interesting to him, and as he grew up a bit, he found himself spending less time with teachers and more time with horses at the Gordon Ranch where you could get a horse for a few hours in exchange for shoveling some horse manure in the stable. When Hugo would see Raphi's grades at school, he would explode, and Raphi would keep quiet. How could he explain to this man who talks about Goethe and Schiller how it feels to ride an Arabian horse on the beach? My guess is that Raphi wasn't too excited about his parents' German passports (although I'm also guessing that he had one himself, but for completely different reasons we'll get to later).

My mom wasn't as enthusiastic about Zionism as Raphi was, and overall, she was on Hugo's side in detaching herself from the mainstream. As a kid, she liked adventures too, but only between the covers of a book. When her brother was chasing camels or riding horses, she would go to a small lending library on Ben Yehuda Street to borrow books in German. When the other kids joined youth movements and went camping, she read *Emil and the Detectives* by Erich Kästner. When her friends joined the *Haganah* (the Jewish paramilitary organization that was fighting the Brits), she read *Winnetou* by Karl May. My mom was an Israeli, and Israel was her home, yet she was always a bit standoffish, a bit of an outsider, and a bit more cosmopolitan than others, so I don't think that she minded whether her parents had passports that were blue, green, or pink.

As a teenager, Raphi joined the *Haganah*, and one night, he volunteered to bring ashore refugees from a ship that had approached Tel Aviv illegally. One of Hugo's acquaintances was also among the volunteers, and the following day he said something that made Hugo understand where Raphi had been the previous night. Hugo was furious. A son of a German lawyer getting involved in illegal activities? He could not accept this. The Brits got the mandate from the League of Nations to rule in Palestine, and we should obey their laws.

I asked Raphi how Oma reacted when she found out that he had joined the *Haganah,* and he said she wasn't too happy about it either. But her discomfort was because it was *gefährlich* (dangerous), not because it was illegal. I doubt that my mom objected to Raphi's participation in a humanitarian act such as bringing refugees to shore, but overall, like Hugo, she saw the law as the absolute most important value, and she was shocked by any deviation, even the slightest one, from the normal social order.

As a kid, I witnessed this whenever I would eat out with my mom and Oma. Lucie had a soft spot for packets of sugar, and she could not leave a restaurant or a café without sliding three or four packets into her purse. After paying the bill, as Lucie would sit and wait for that special moment when all the waiters were in the kitchen, my mother (who knew it was coming) would warn her: "*Mutti!*" to which Oma would respond: "Mirjam!" Next, my mom would try to reason with her, or look up to the ceiling and start a conversation with "*Gott*" (God, in whose existence she did not believe). Nothing made a difference. At the right moment (and that moment always came—I think that many waiters fully cooperated with Lucie who was a generous tipper), Lucie would open the clasp, and in a split second, the loot would lie at the bottom of her purse.

Like her father, my mom was also repulsed by radicalism and violence. Years later, she would find out that the attack that had accidentally killed the young Jewish radio announcer had been planned by one of our acquaintances as part of his activities against the Brits. My mom refused to ever shake that man's hand.

In 1933, before my family left Germany, it was my Zionist grandfather Hugo who pushed for going to Tel Aviv and my grandmother Lucie who wasn't too excited. Yet somehow the roles switched in Israel, and Lucie became the Israeli. Now in

Düsseldorf, Hugo and Lucie fully agreed on one thing: They were tired. The past two decades had made them tired. So once they had their passports, they were ready to leave for Wiesbaden. To rest, "that's what we came here for," Lucie wrote. "To rest from 23 years of heat and hardship." And a couple of days after getting the passports, they were on the train to Wiesbaden.

16 WIESBADEN
"THEY ALL KNEW EACH OTHER."

As my train leaves Düsseldorf, I'm trying to guess whether the hotel in Wiesbaden would accommodate my whimsical request to stay in the same room my grandparents had stayed in in 1956. I know it's crazy, but hey, this is Germany, and they keep good records. Besides, the hotel has been under the same management of the Bödeker family. It's not impossible.

Hugo wrote that he felt as if he were entering a time machine as they boarded the train, and now I understand what he meant. At first, the train goes through residential sections of Düsseldorf, but then buildings are replaced by trees and later by an occasional old castle or a fort in the forest I'm sure hasn't changed throughout the past 100 years. Lucie was impressed by how well he remembered all the stops. After Düsseldorf, he knew that they would reach Cologne, and after Cologne, Bonn, and after Bonn, Koblenz. And by the Lorelei cliff, Lucie remembered the famous lines from Heinrich Heine's poem: "I don't know what it could mean, or why I am so sad." But Lucie wrote that she *did* know why she was sad—because we were not there with her.

There's a picture in my living room that was taken by my grandfather Hugo on that dream vacation in Wiesbaden in 1925. It's a photo of the three women in his life: his daughter, Mirjam; his wife, Lucie; and his sister, Liese (who had joined them on that trip). It always strikes me how, as they look at the camera, the women in the picture can't imagine what is about to unfold in the next few decades and with how much dedication and love the little girl would take care of the older two. And another thing happens when I look at this picture: I feel for the photographer. I have not met (at least so far) a single person who has told me that he loved Hugo— not Martin in Los Angeles, not Gertrud Katz in New York, not Ruth, not even Raphi, his son. But looking at the expressions on their faces, the three women in the picture seemed to love him, and they open a tiny door to him in my heart.

* * *

They arrived in Wiesbaden on Friday, August 24th, 1956, at 3 p.m.—two German citizens who no longer needed to get a visa to enter their country. It was drizzling outside, and they took a cab to the hotel.

When I arrive, the sun is shining. The clerk at Hotel Bären greets me with a wide smile. His skin is very dark, and his black hair is neatly combed to the side. He's expecting me. Mrs. Bödeker had to leave to run some errands, but she asked to let me know that no, they don't know in what room my grandparents had stayed. However, they have an idea of where it might have been. The problem is that I asked for a non-smoking room, and this is in the smoking section; do I still want to sleep in the room?

He hands me a heavy key, (the type they used to have in all hotels), and I go upstairs to my room (perhaps their room) on the second floor. I unlock the heavy door with my heavy key, only to find another heavy door in front of me. Everything is done to ensure that guests will not be disturbed. The room behind that second door is small and friendly, and it welcomes me with a pleasant scent of wood furniture. It is different from American hotel rooms: there is no built-in closet, but rather a wooden wardrobe as in

Oma's apartment. The bed is small, and the curtains with green and yellow stripes filter the light coming through the window. Only now I start to understand where Hugo and Lucie got the idea that they were going to Germany to rest. The hotel welcomed them with a promise of comfort. An elevator would take them directly to the thermal pool in the basement. There, in the private little bathtubs that are fed by the hotel's own spring, the special water would comfort their spirit and their bones. And the lady in white who prepared the bath for them would also prepare a warm towel that would be waiting for them when they got out.

I put on a bathrobe, take the elevator down to the pool, and I get into the water. It is hot and comforting. I'm the only one in the large room, and the high ceiling echoes the splutter of the water. I can feel my leg muscles relaxing. I have read on the train about the healing properties of the minerals in Wiesbaden water. Something about salts, sulfate, silica, and toxins that are released from one's body. I float and close my eyes. It's quiet, and part of me is embarrassed by my arrogance—that I did not believe that they came here to recover. They were brought up in Germany with the idea of *Kur*—that when you are exhausted, you rejuvenate at a spa. They believed in the healing power of soaking in hot springs, and when Hugo was falling apart, this was the solution that came to mind.

The following day I meet with Mrs. Bödeker who runs the hotel. She has a pretty face surrounded by gray hair. Her mother, a bigger woman with white hair who ran the hotel back in 1956, joins us.

"Do you have a picture of your grandparents?" the older Mrs. Bödeker asks.

I run back to my room to get a photograph. No, she doesn't recognize them. Definitely not Hugo. Maybe Lucie. Do I remember any other of their friends? I remember that they mentioned an acquaintance named Julius Simon who also stayed at the hotel, and this name ignites a spark in the older woman's eyes.

"Oh, yes! I remember Dr. Simon. They used to come here a lot!" she says.

It's the first time that I feel comfortable on this trip. Maybe it's the warmth projected by the younger Mrs. Bödeker who lived in San Francisco for a couple of years in the 1970s. Maybe it's the fact that the older Mrs. Bödeker tells me how all the *Yekkes* from Tel Aviv used to come here.

"They all knew each other," she says, "and they all told each other about this place."

It feels good to be with these two ladies, but I'm also disappointed. On my way to my room to get the picture, I thought, "What a surprise! I finally meet someone who was here with my grandparents!" Maybe the older Bödeker knows something. Perhaps when she sees my grandfather Hugo's picture, she'll say, "Oh sure, I recognize him. I remember that we called a doctor after he went wild in the dining room." Or maybe after she sees Lucie's picture, she'll say: "Yes, one night I couldn't sleep, and I walked around the hotel, and your grandmother was sitting in the lobby, and I had a conversation with her that I will never forget—we sat in the lobby for two hours and talked about everything."

But no, she does not recognize them.

The younger Mrs. Bödeker and I go outside to the street. She tells me that the alley behind the hotel was destroyed during the war. The hotel itself was partially ruined and was rebuilt. There have been additional changes since the 50s, and Mrs. Bödeker outlines them one by one so that I can imagine exactly how it all looked when my grandparents were here. She and her brother grew up in the hotel, and she remembers hiding behind corners and niches in the corridors and jumping in front of guests lost in their thoughts. She had a happy childhood here. We avoid what Germans and Jews usually avoid. When she talks about the bombing or when I talk about my grandparents, we're both just two archeologists visiting an ancient site. She tells me how each guest had his or her napkin that they kept throughout their stay and their regular table. You could take full-board (*Vollpension*) or half-board (*Halbpension*). Most people took the full board because it made more sense than *Halbpension*, Mrs. Bödeker explains, and when she says *Halbpension* again, I hear my mom saying that word in her daily phone conversation with Oma, and I miss them terribly, especially my mom.[1]

* * *

I'm sure that having their regular table with their regular napkins gave Lucie and Hugo great comfort, and so did the strict adherence to proper placement of utensils and glassware—identical to the order they followed in their meals at home and their *Kaffee und Kuchen* (coffee and cake) ritual on their balcony in Tel Aviv. They loved the rituals of meals, and in later years, my mom and Oma made it their life goals to teach Eva and me good table manners: don't chew with your mouth open, don't make any noise, don't slurp, no elbows on the table, use a salad fork for the salad, never cut a potato with a knife, and never ever put a knife in your mouth. Here too, an arsenal of sayings boosted the ritual. My mom couldn't serve soup without saying, "*Mit Suppe wartet man nicht*" (one does not wait with soup). At the end of the meal, we had to ask, "May I get up?" (in German or Hebrew), and my mom's canned response was (always in German) "*Mach dass du wegkommst*" (make yourself disappear). When she would serve chicken drumsticks, my mom would give us the green light to pick them up with our hands because "even the queen does it," referring to some magazine article Oma had read that Queen Elizabeth had eaten a drumstick at a picnic without a fork and a knife. Incidentally, that last saying taught me that there's some flexibility when it comes to table manners, and today (only when I'm by myself), after I spread a slice of bread with something that I particularly like (like Trader Joe's Goat's Milk Creamy Cheese), I put the knife in my mouth and clean it up in one sweep like a sword swallower at the end of his show.

Then I look up, wink at my mom, and see her covering her eyes, shaking her head, laughing and begging, "Enough!"

17 WIESBADEN

"VATI IS ONCE AGAIN THE GENTLEMAN HE USED TO BE."

When Lucie and Hugo woke up on Saturday morning, Wiesbaden smiled at them. The sun was shining, and they took the bus to the base of Neroberg, the hill above the city. They bought a ticket for the cable car that would take them to the top of the hill and waited like kids before a ride in an amusement park. At the top of the hill, there's an identical cable car now filled with 7,000 liters of water. When its container is full, the driver releases the brakes, and the car starts sliding downhill. A metal cable connects the two cars, so when the heavy car slides down, it pulls its light partner. Then the roles change: The car at the bottom releases its water, and a pump sends the water uphill into the other car.[1]

I'm sitting in the car at the bottom that is ready to start climbing. It stands on a slope. The driver in blue overalls closes the doors and says something to the walkie-talkie he is holding in his hand, and the yellow car starts climbing up the hill. Because it doesn't have an engine, you hear only squeaks and click-clacks of gears. Beech trees and ancient oaks shed a shadow over the car. Everything is green and safe. The car that is traveling downhill passes my car. Maybe a little girl waved at my grandparents, as she does to me now.

I suddenly realize that I don't have any pictures from their 1956 trip. All the pictures I have from Wiesbaden were taken in 1925. People tend to take pictures of their happiness, and maybe Hugo left his camera in Tel Aviv because he didn't expect any happy moments. But there were some. They walked around the garden at the top of the hill. Their original plan included drinking coffee in the restaurant there, but it was too crowded. The weather was nice, and the path that leads to the forest winked at them with an old friend's smile: You remember that one can go down on foot. My grandfather Hugo was 65 and my grandmother Lucie 58, but they decided to do it like they had 31 years ago. The walk downhill is not short, and what they did with no effort three decades earlier was not easy now.

"If it weren't so sad, you would have laughed too if you saw us waddling downhill," Lucie wrote to my mother. But despite the difficulty, it seems that this path took them back to their Germany. Neither of them remembered how beautiful the forest was. "The forest is charming," Lucie wrote. If only they could pack the forest and take it back to Israel. "But, *Oy Vey*, I haven't thought about customs," Lucie added (now she was peppering her letter with Yiddish, not a trivial thing for a *Yekke*).

Here they are–I see them waddling down the hill. I can imagine them laughing. Maybe they even call each other with a yoo-hoo like in the good old days, and their yodel that echoes throughout the forest comes back to them: "Doctor and Frau Doctor Mendel! We haven't seen you for ages! Welcome back!" Another cable car loaded with people slides downhill past them, but they don't care that others will arrive before them. They will do it at their own pace. They are *zufrieden* (content).

Wiesbaden was good to them, as on that vacation back in 1925, and true joy started to bubble up through their letters. Hugo teased Lucie that with the excess weight building under her clothes, they wouldn't let her go through customs without a body search. And she said, in her defense, that the food is so good here and the portions huge. And a few days later, Lucie wrote to my mother, "*Vati* (dad) is once again the gentleman he used to be." And she noted how well he was finding his way around Wiesbaden. The coffee that they meant to drink at the top of Neroberg wasn't forgotten of course. They drank it at Café Blum that they called in their letters *Stammcafé* (our regular place).

18 WIESBADEN
"ONCE YOU'VE LEARNED SOMETHING ..."

It's a beautiful day. Café Blum is surrounded by purple flags announcing its 125th anniversary, and I'm sitting at one of the tables on the sidewalk. A man in a fancy suit is sitting at the table next to me, a handkerchief sticking out of his front pocket. He doesn't seem to know anyone here. Just reading the paper. At the table on my other side sit four elegantly dressed older women. Another woman passes by on the sidewalk, and they all greet her. She says something short and apparently witty, without even slowing down, and they all burst into laughter. I couldn't hear what she said, but something in her dialect and tone that lingers in the air makes me feel at home.

A waitress with round glasses clears the plates of the four women at the next table, stacking the dishes into an unstable tower, and I hear my mom's voice in my head: *Gelernt ist gelernt* (once you've learned something ...). As a teenager, Raphi started to work as a "Piccolo" (a waiter's assistant), and after a week at work, he wanted to demonstrate his new skill. So after dinner, he proudly stacked all the family's plates on one hand, and when Lucie said how impressed she was, he said, *"Gelernt ist gelernt,"* turned around, and all the dishes smashed onto the floor. I heard *"Gelernt ist gelernt"* any time I carried more than one plate to the kitchen.

Cafés and waiters played a central role in our family lore. In addition to *"Gelernt ist gelernt,"* my mom and Oma had several other sayings in this domain. For example, if my sister or I sang at the dinner table, my mom would scold us, saying "This is not a *Musikcafé!*" If a waiter were slow to serve us, or made a serious mistake, they would whisper to us: "He won't last to serve matzo balls here." And when Oma would steal sugar packets, she would say, "It's been paid for already."

Yesterday I walked around the garden behind the *Kurhaus* (the landmark spa house and convention center). At the café in that garden, my grandparents had coffee too, and they reminded my mom in their letter of how she had thrown up chocolate pudding with whipped cream there in 1925. It occurs to me that mine was the second family pilgrimage to the puking site. (A little brass plaque may be appropriate: "Here, in 1925, the girl Mirjam Mendel threw up her chocolate pudding and whipped cream.")

It isn't a coincidence that they were so preoccupied with cafés. In some ways, it was their battlefield—where they moved from one side of the table to the other and back—from guests to servers to guests. When Hugo was a successful lawyer in Hamm, they were regulars in some cafés in town. About a year after they got to Palestine, they opened a café on Ben Yehuda Street, which became another part of their bumpy history in Tel Aviv. At first, Café Mendel seemed to be a source of pride and joy. They were now owners of two businesses: a small factory and a café. Pictures from that time show them sitting around a table *zufrieden* or Lucie clearing the dishes with a smile. But my mom always told me how difficult those years were for Lucie who slaved in the kitchen from the early hours of the morning until late at night. I suspect that the economic depression didn't skip Café Mendel, and after four years, the café closed.[1] Lucie started working behind the counter at Café Palatin on Ahad Ha'Am Street. Now she wasn't a business owner any longer, but an employee, and Hugo didn't like that she was serving their acquaintances from the old country. Even to those who didn't know about the problems with the wire business, this café job announced that the Mendels weren't doing too well.

The man in the fancy suit at the table next to me has a visitor now. A woman approaches him, and they start chatting like old friends. Am I the only one who's lonely here?

19 WIESBADEN
"THOSE DAMN GUILTY FEELINGS."

One evening after dinner at Hotel Bären, Hugo said that he had eaten too much and was going for a walk. Lucie noted in her letter that he had taken one of my mom's letters with him. I come along. I see him on *Bärenstraße*, right by the hotel. Over there, by the street light, a couple is hugging. When he passes by, he hears a giggle. It's raining, and people are rushing home, people from Wiesbaden whose homes are in Wiesbaden. People who do not know any other version of life but this one.

I know how much Hugo missed her now, walking in the dark, clutching her letter in his hand. As a four-year-old, my mom's favorite thing was to sit at his office and ask about the different letters on the typewriter.

"What is this one, *Vati* (dad)?"

"It is an M," her *Vati* answers.

"Am I allowed to press it?"

"Yes," Hugo says, and she hits the key so lightly that no letter appears on the paper.

"Press harder!" Hugo tells her, and she does. Nothing.

"Even harder," Hugo says, and she hits the key with one fierce little finger.

"Look *Vati*, M!" she cries, and she sees her dad smiling.

Soon she knew where the I and the R and the J and the A were. And one day she typed her name: MIRJAM. And in the months that followed, when they would walk together on the street, he would quiz her on street signs.

"A-P-O-T-H-E-K-E," she adds the letters and tries to decipher the code.

"Yes, my child, what is it?" he asks.

She struggles, but suddenly everything makes sense. "*Apotheke!*" (pharmacy) she exclaims, and her father smiles again.

In the fall, at the age of four and a half, Mirjam started reading books. And thus my mom was introduced to the two things she would need in this world: the typewriter that would bring food to our table and the book that would transport her to other worlds. Yet back in the 1920s, her smarts inspired bigger dreams in Hugo's mind. The year she was born, 1922, was the first year women could practice law in Germany, and when she was just ten years old, he taught her whole paragraphs from the German Civil Code (that she could still recite as an adult). It was clear to him that she would become a lawyer one day herself and that she would join him as his partner. It was clear to her too. Their dream did not die even after they'd moved to Tel Aviv. When she ran out of children's books in German to read in the small lending library, she would open one of the few law books that he had brought along and ask him questions about German law. And how proud was he when she started her law studies at the University of London's extension in Tel Aviv.

* * *

Once when I visited my mom in Tel Aviv, we were going somewhere together in her car. She was driving, and I was sitting next to her when we stopped at a light. We were talking about her parents. I can't remember what we'd been saying when she suddenly burst into tears: "Those damn guilty feelings," she cried, and hit the steering wheel with her fist again and again and again. Then the light turned green, and she drove as if nothing had happened. As much as I asked, she refused to go back to the subject.

20 FRANKFURT

"ARE YOU MIRJAM MENDEL'S DAD?"

Mary Fürstenberg, Hugo's cousin from Frankfurt, had been searching for Hugo and Lucie since the day they'd arrived in Germany. From the letter they had sent from Tel Aviv, she knew that they would be in Düsseldorf, and she asked her husband, Franz, to check with likely local hotels, but to no avail. On Monday morning, when she got a postcard from Hugo that they were now in Wiesbaden, she immediately looked for Franz's driver who would take her there, and when she couldn't find him, she got on the bus and showed up at their hotel at noon.

A petite woman, wearing a fashionable dress to her knees, and exceptionally quiet, she was immediately classified by Lucie as *"Hat viel mitgemacht"* (had been through a lot) based on the torturous times they had gone through in Manila under Japanese occupation. At first, the Japanese saw the German Jews who'd escaped to Manila as simply Germans—people with a swastika in their passports, which meant they were allies. After some time, the Japanese soldiers learned the meaning of the big letter "J" that was stamped in those passports, but they still treated people reasonably well. Things turned hellish when General Douglas MacArthur tried to deliver on his famous promise to recapture Manila ("I shall return"). Then the Japanese army went wild, killing thousands of civilians and systematically burning sections of the city while the Americans were bombing it. What exactly happened to Mary during that time wasn't clear, but the woman who was always a quiet person was now almost whispering. Here in Germany, she said that everyone was looking at her. After Manila, they lived in Sydney, Australia, which was her favorite place, but Franz's work and his longing for Europe dictated their location.

Lucie was impressed by how Mary looked and took care of herself. "She probably thinks that I'm a fat farmer's wife," Lucie wrote and complained that she already weighed 69 kilos. "But *Ein Davar*," (never mind) she switched to Hebrew again, "I'll have plenty of opportunities to shed those extra kilos." Mary served as a reference point for Lucie in another respect: "People like Mary have kind of an inferiority complex next to the *Goyim*," she wrote, as opposed to "us Israelis" who are much more self-assured and straightforward as Jews.

On Saturday, Mary came back with Franz in his company car, and they took the Mendels to Rüdesheim, a romantic wine village by the Rhine River. Franz, a tall man with two deep wrinkles around his mouth, drove along the river. Before the war, he worked as an executive in the film company UFA in Berlin. When they escaped to Manila, he used his connections to start an advertising business in movie theaters. Business was good, and he also did well in Sydney and London right after the war. Now he managed the rental business for Metro, but he wasn't too happy there and was thinking of his next move. "A big man," Hugo commented, and I imagine him sitting in the back of the car, head down, listening to the stories of the man who had succeeded on three continents.[1]

On Sunday at ten in the morning, Lucie and Hugo got on a bus for Frankfurt, but when they said "bus," Lucie clarified that they were not talking about a crowded, noisy, Israeli bus with hard wooden benches but a German bus with soft seats and pre-war politeness. The moment they left Wiesbaden, they were sucked into what

Hugo described as a human whirlpool of cars and people on the highway. "You can't imagine the traffic!" he wrote to my mom.

At 11:30, they arrived at the apartment of Hilde and Ernst Katzenstein for a get together with three couples, which included the Katzensteins, the Herzfelds, and the Fürstenbergs. The hosts, the Katzensteins, were old acquaintances whom Lucie and Hugo had known through Lucie's sister, Käthe. Ernst Katzenstein, a relatively short and round-faced lawyer from Jerusalem, was, as mentioned earlier, the director of the Jewish Claims Conference in Germany.[2] His wife, Hilde, was relatively short too, and Lucie reported that she was not getting any younger but that her face was pretty as before. And Lucie thought that the Katzenstein's apartment was tastefully designed. Even though some of the furniture had come with the place, the design seemed so personal that even Mary and Franz Fürstenberg, who had seen some fancy houses in their lifetime, agreed with her.

Hepps Herzfeld was Lucie's cousin, and Lucie wrote that she was dressed elegantly but that all the ornaments in the world couldn't hide the fact that she didn't look healthy. Her arthritis was killing her, and she asked to tell everyone who complained that she wasn't writing that this was the only reason—she couldn't even hold a pen. Manfred Herzfeld, Hepps' husband, was a short bald man with thick glasses who always walked around with a cane for extra effect. He now worked for the JRSO in Berlin (The JRSO, Jewish Restitution Successor Organization, represented large Jewish organizations in their dealings with West Germany). Lucie wrote that he remained the same absent-minded professor he used to be but that he looked good and was as mentally active as before.

With the Fürstenbergs and the Mendels, they were eight altogether, eight souls blasted from Germany in all directions after the big bang—the Katzensteins to Jerusalem, London, and Frankfurt, the Fürstenbergs to Manila and then Sydney and Frankfurt, the Herzfelds to Jerusalem and then to Berlin, and the Mendels to Tel Aviv. Now I imagine that these eight splinters were comparing notes over lunch: What happened to the Schwartz family? And the Steiners? When certain last names were mentioned, eyes went down. When certain places were brought up, maybe someone choked up. Perhaps Lucie burst out of the room when someone asked about Northeim.

And what about Ilse, Manfred Herzfeld's sister? Oh, she met this American author, William S. Burroughs, who married her before the war so that she could get a green card, and she now lives in New York. And Hugo, how is your sister, Liese, doing? She is *zufrieden* but is still trying to divorce that taxi driver who charmed her and then left Tel Aviv for Frankfurt. Hugo is going to contact a local lawyer named Alexander Besser to handle the case. He came with high recommendations from a friend in Tel Aviv. Besser? What a small world! Ernst Katzenstein and Manfred Herzfeld know him from their work.

Lucie reported in her letter that Katzenstein had made an offer to Hugo to call Besser right then, and after Hugo introduced himself on the phone, it sounded like the name Hugo Mendel rang a bell at the other end of the line. Why not? After all, Hugo was a successful lawyer in the old days, authorized to appear in the higher regional court.

"Are you Mirjam Mendel's dad?" Besser asked. It turns out that he had known Mirjam from his years in Tel Aviv. Yes, he too escaped to the Holy Land, albeit much later than Dr. Mendel, and when he had lived there, he had the pleasure of knowing Mirjam. "How is she doing?"

"You used to be Hugo Mendel's daughter," Lucie wrote to my mom, "and now Dad is Mirjam Mendel's father."

After the afternoon coffee, the eight still sat and schmoozed until it began to get dark, and the Katzensteins drove the Herzfelds to the airport where they would catch their flight to Berlin, and Mary and Franz drove the Mendels to the bus station. At 7 p.m., Hugo and Lucie were on the bus back to Wiesbaden, and I think that my grandpa Hugo was quiet, as you may expect from someone who had just met some alternative versions of his life.

Before the war, Ernst Katzenstein was a Jewish lawyer in the German town of Hamelin, where Käthe, Lucie's sister, lived with her husband, Harry Binheim, who was a lawyer too. In 1933, when Jewish lawyers could no longer appear in court in Germany, Katzenstein immigrated to Palestine, just like Hugo, but he was 35, seven years younger than Hugo, and he had no family. He studied for the exams for foreign lawyers and passed them successfully. He wasn't satisfied with a license to practice law as an advocate and traveled to England for a couple of years to study for additional exams that would make him a barrister, allowed to appear in the higher court. In the summer of 1939, he returned to Jerusalem and became a successful lawyer in town. After the war, the Jewish Agency sent him to Germany to handle reparations and restitution issues, and just a few months before Hugo and Lucie's visit, he became the head of the Claims Conference in Germany.

Perhaps Manfred Herzfeld's story was at the forefront of Hugo's mind that evening on their bus ride back to Wiesbaden. While Katzenstein was younger, and always on top, Manfred Herzfeld was seven years older than Hugo and had managed a nice comeback. Before the war, Herzfeld was a lawyer in Celle and, like Hugo, was authorized to appear in the Higher Regional Court. The rules against Jewish lawyers affected his economic situation dramatically, and in 1935, he moved to Jerusalem with Hepps and their daughter, Eva. Here, in a basement apartment, the family tried to get back on their feet. Manfred got a job as a cashier at an insurance company, which was hardly intellectually satisfying for a man who would go home to write poetry and read philosophy and literature in Greek and Latin. In 1950, when Katzenstein invited him to go back to Germany and work for the JRSO, Manfred was torn. On the one hand, he vowed never to go back to Germany. On the other hand, the opportunity to work again in his beloved profession was too hard to resist.

Perhaps Manfred's story should have given Hugo hope. Maybe Hugo was hoping that Katzenstein would ask him to join them too. I don't know what was going on in my grandfather Hugo's mind. It was probably like the whirlpool on the highway outside the bus window, with streams of vehicles flowing in all directions. Maybe the idea of working as a lawyer scared him. If he got a second chance, would he be up to the challenge? Was he as mentally active as Herzfeld was? What if he got confused on his way to work? And could he get over his disgust with the way the German legal system had not stood up to the Nazis? Manfred Herzfeld too had strong feelings against the German judges who had "turned justice into a prostitute of politics," as he wrote in a poem right after the war. Were the German judges different now? Could Hugo see himself standing in a German court again?[3]

A couple of nights earlier, Lucie and Hugo watched the movie *Serenade* with the famous singer Mario Lanza. It's the story of Damon Vincenti, a poor vineyard worker in Southern California with a golden voice and dreams of becoming an operatic tenor. Damon finds his way to San Francisco where he gets a job as a singer and falls in love with a high society hostess, Kendall Hale. He keeps developing as a tenor, and his success brings him and Kendall to New York City where he starts rehearsing for the role of Othello in a big production. But he also starts suspecting that Kendall is having an affair with a local sculptor, and on opening night, when Damon realizes that the seat he reserved for her is empty, he removes his makeup and runs to their apartment, where all he finds is a still-wet sculpture of his love, Kendall.

With his US career ruined after such irresponsible behavior, Damon auditions in Mexico City where he hopes to get a second chance. The eyes of the Mexican director and producer are on him as he tries to sing, but he chokes. He apologizes and starts again, but his voice isn't what it used to be. The producer and director don't even have to tell him what they think. He understands.

Lucie wrote that Hugo was especially moved by this film.

21 WIESBADEN
"I'M NOT GOING TO FAST FOR THREE MARKS."

Lucie and Hugo were back in their hotel by 8:15 p.m. and had dinner at their own personal table with their own personal napkins. When did Hugo's darkness start? Not the usual darkness, but darkness so deep that it makes someone want to smash into the pavement? Everywhere I go in this hotel, I can't help but look for places from which Hugo may have considered jumping. On my first day here, as I walked downstairs, I noticed that the stairwell was wide enough for someone to jump. Was he contemplating it here already, or did the idea come to him later on the trip? Or was it something that popped into his mind in Tel Aviv only upon their return?

Or maybe the idea emerged in their little apartment before the trip? There's a moment in a person's life (not a simple moment) when other people no longer pester him. A person needs people to tug at his sleeve, to want something, to be nagged a bit. And if he always (and not just before nap time as my mom did) orders his family to tell anyone who calls that he is dead, then fewer and fewer people call. And if the man is too proud to pick up the phone and call a friend, a moment arises at which no one calls anymore. Back then, there was no phone at their apartment, so it was even easier for Hugo to shut himself up: not to respond when invited for coffee, not to invite others, not to answer when the doorbell rings. An image pops into my mind of Hugo sitting in bed in buttoned-up pajamas, and the doorbell rings and rings and rings.

* * *

During breakfast the following day here in Wiesbaden, Hugo was called to the phone. It was Alexander Besser, yet another rendition of his life—another German Jewish lawyer who had fled to Tel Aviv with little command of English or Hebrew. Unlike Hugo, Besser was never a Zionist, so he didn't even consider becoming a lawyer in Palestine. Tel Aviv for him was an awning under which you hide during a storm. He supported himself by writing for a local newspaper in German, and he liked playing the piano in bars and cafés. In 1950, when the sky had cleared, Besser returned to Germany, got his license back, and ran a successful law practice in Frankfurt.

They agreed that Besser would come to Wiesbaden later in the week to discuss the situation with Hugo's sister, Liese, and her divorce from the big cab driver who now lived in Frankfurt, but Besser came to Wiesbaden the following day. He arrived by bus, a small man with a handsome head covered by a fedora. He said he had only an hour, and they sat down at a small café and went right to business, not before he asked how Raphi was doing, which Lucie said was a distraction tactic because right after that question, he started asking about Mirjam and did not stop. As far as Liese's husband was concerned, Besser promised to talk with him firmly, and Hugo wrote that he wasn't too optimistic, maybe basing his assessment on a physical match between the big cab driver and the tiny lawyer. Lucie wrote that Besser impressed her as a very serious man.[1]

As my mom was reading their reports, she probably brushed off her mother's insinuations regarding any romantic relationships with Besser (He was 20 years her senior). I suspect that she was much more concerned about her father and how the encounters with alternative scenarios of his life were affecting him. And maybe she was inventing happy endings in her head—new possible twists in his story. What if Ernst Katzenstein offered her dad a job? What if her father met one of his old-time colleagues who then took him as a partner? Or what if he found a way to reopen his office in Hamm? All he needed was a small office, a desk, and new letterhead. Didn't he deserve it?

Her hopes for him, I'm sure, were not without ambivalence—she would miss her parents terribly if they returned to Germany–and not without apprehension when she thought about his mental state and how he had become the client of his former colleagues. Dr. Robert Gidion, who had emigrated in 1933 from Cologne to Tel Aviv, was now the liquidator of Hugo's company. The lawyer Friedrich Kieserling from Hamm helped Hugo secure a monthly allowance for the loss of his profession, which was welcomed, of course, but also in some ways sealed the loss of his honor. And even though my mother was hoping for an optimistic twist in his story, she knew other versions very well. A few years earlier, my mom's uncle Harry Binheim who had been a lawyer in Hamelin (like Katzenstein) died heartbroken in the small village in Israel where he and Käthe (Oma's sister) lived.[2] And there was Dr. Samuelsdorff, who had tried a comeback a couple of years before Hugo and Lucie's trip. In 1954, Dr. Erich Samuelsdorff returned from Tel Aviv to Hamm and tried to reestablish his law practice. He needed a small loan to start the business, and as the loan approval was slow to arrive, he found himself in a small apartment, waiting, and he ended up dying of a heart attack on his birthday, just days before the green light from the bank arrived.[3] My grandfather Hugo Mendel was now walking in single file behind thousands of other Jewish lawyers, as an invisible finger was pointing them left to life, or right to death.

My mom herself was now working as a secretary for a lanky German-born lawyer by the name of Erwin Lichtenstein in Tel Aviv, one of those who were pointed to the left—to life.

Lichtenstein, who was eight years younger than Hugo, was fluent in Hebrew and German and ran a successful practice on Allenby Street. Back in 1933, when he could no longer appear in court in Germany, he became the counsel for the Jewish Community in Danzig. After he immigrated to Israel, he passed the exams, and he now specialized in restitution for the Jews of the city of Danzig that had some unique legal issues because of the city's semiautonomous status before the war.[4]

With a note pad in her hand, my mom would walk into Dr. Lichtenstein's office and take dictation, and I imagine him walking back and forth dictating his letters, and not only is his body lanky but also his head is long and tilted a bit. I'm sure that as she was jotting down her wild stenographic notes (which she alone could decipher), she always had this in the back of her mind: "This could have been my dad," or "I remember when dad explained to me this exact same legal concept." And later, as she would type the letter back at her desk, she would perhaps think, "My dad could have done this. He can do this. Maybe it's not too late."

There was a time my mother hoped to save her father's honor with her own hands, and for a moment in 1948, it looked like she was on her way to becoming a lawyer herself. A decade or so earlier, in 1939, Mirjam announced one day that she was quitting high school and switching to a vocational school to learn stenography and typing. Her parents tried to talk her out of it. She had such a bright future ahead of her, and no university would accept her without her having graduated from a regular high school.

But Mirjam was determined to quit school. She could no longer sit in literature and history classes without helping her parents. She saw the daily pain of their economic fall. She heard their fights. They were now sleeping in two separate rooms—Hugo in the same room as Raphi and Lucie in the same room as she. And Mirjam saw her mom waking up in the early hours of the morning to start the 6 a.m. shift at Café Palatin and her dad doing his rounds to hardware stores and then sitting at the storage yard, surrounded by piles of barbed wire. So she switched to a vocational school, and a few months later, she found a job as a typist for one of the *Yekke* lawyers in town and started to contribute to the family budget.

Without a high school diploma, she did not think she would ever be able to study law, but in 1945, Mirjam found out about an alternative: passing the matriculation exam of the University of London would allow her to study at its extension in Tel Aviv. Mirjam dove into math, English, and economics books for several months and passed the exams successfully. With this under her belt, she signed up for night classes at the University of London extension in Tel Aviv and was now a law student. In January 1948, when she received a telegram from London that she had passed the intermediate exam in law, she was almost as proud as her dad.

But other things happened in 1948. In May, the British Mandate over Palestine ended, the State of Israel was declared, and the War of Independence started. My mom was recruited as a typist to the supreme command of the young Israeli Army, where she met a young officer named Yehuda Rosen. Once the war was over, everything was different: studying law was possible only at one of the Israeli universities, and entering any of these schools required a regular high school diploma. When Eva was born, the dream became even less realistic. When I was born, the dream nearly evaporated. When my father died eight months later, the dream died with him.

* * *

One day, as Lucie and Hugo were sitting at Café Blum for their regular afternoon coffee, and just as they thought that Wiesbaden was *judenrein* ("cleansed of Jews"—Lucie sarcastically used the Nazi term), they saw another couple from Tel Aviv—the Alexanders. "If we were in Tel Aviv, I would not have made myself so visible," Lucie wrote, "but here I jumped as if bitten by a tarantula." The Alexanders joined their table and told them they were staying at a nearby town named Königstein im Taunus and that the Mendels *must* come to see its beauty.

A couple of days later, Hugo and Lucie took the bus, and the city charmed them as promised, especially the Taunus forest around it. But this visit again brought out Lucie's rage at Germany. It helped her understand how much they had lost in the past few decades, she explained. She just hoped that her loved ones would be able to see this beauty one day. Lucie herself was surprised by the jealousy and hate bubbling in her and said she wasn't proud of this side of her personality. (When I visit Königstein im Taunus, it becomes pretty clear to me why Lucie's rage resurfaced here. A perfumery owner, who knows the local history, tells me that only two or three houses were destroyed in the bombing during the war, which means that this town looked a lot like the Germany Lucie had known before the war.)

Her emotional turmoil was now combined with total detachment from the German way of life. She was tired of anything German. The constant greetings *"Guten Abend, guten Tag, guten Morgen, guten Appetit"* (good evening, good day, good morning, good meal) were getting on her nerves, and she referred to the Germans' habit of greeting strangers on the street as stupidity. Even the concerts in the Kurhaus garden that she and Hugo once loved so much she now called *"ein grosses Goyim naches"* (a big gentiles' pleasure.[5])

Not that she had much patience for Jewish habits. The following day was Yom Kippur, and when Mrs. Alexander asked her whether she was going to fast, Oma calculated that she would save three German Marks if she did.

"I'm not going to fast for three marks," Lucie said, and everybody laughed.

This rebellious attitude towards religion (and certainly against religious coercion) was part of their way of life, of our way of life. The only time of the year that my mom would bake bread was during Passover because the stores wouldn't sell it. Hugo was more militant on this front, and he was known to sit on their balcony on Yom Kippur and eat grapes. Kind of a tradition. One grape after the other, he would pop into his mouth, and Lucie would try to convince him to come in. No need to upset people. But the grapes were good, and Hugo was stubborn. Stubborn and a lawyer with a deep awareness of civil rights, and as is well known, everybody is entitled to do what he wishes in the privacy of his home, within the parameters of the law of course. And as far as he knew, there was no civil law forbidding people from eating on Yom Kippur.

* * *

On my last evening in Wiesbaden, I go for one final stroll in town. There's a drizzle. My legs take me to Café Blum, my regular place. The waitress with the glasses who served me several times previously is busy chaining the chairs outside. No, they're not closing, but nobody's going to sit outside in the rain. I sit down and order potato soup, perfect for this weather. My mom used to make potato soup so thick that I would make roads in it with a tablespoon and drive those roads to faraway places before they would slowly close on themselves. But the soup that arrives is different, much thinner, with sausage.

When I leave Café Blum, two young women dressed in black approach me. One of them, carrying a large camera, asks me in English how to get to some movie theater. I notice her heavy Israeli accent and ask if she speaks Hebrew. She does. A bit surprised, she explains that they are in a hurry. A film that they made is being presented at some festival. It must be around here somewhere. Do I know where it is? I ask if they have a map. They do, but they don't know what street the theater is on. It's a small theater, an art house. Do I know where it is? I don't. I ask them about the film, but they don't have time for the guy who's asking so many questions, and they run away—two black silhouettes in the rain, and a man with an umbrella watching them run off, longing for thick potato soup.

When my mom told me about the suicide, she said that Hugo missed Germany, but it didn't register with me, which is surprising because I know something about longing. I'm an immigrant, too, although far different from Hugo. (I wasn't forced out of my country. The Gestapo never showed up at my doorstep. I was never persecuted.) Somehow, even though she said that he missed Germany, something in me could not accept that anyone would miss Germany after everything that had happened here. The problem was that I wasn't thinking of all the different flavors of missing. When I miss Israel, I don't necessarily miss today's Israel but the Israel of my childhood and people like my mom and Oma. It's such an obvious point, but somehow I didn't see that Hugo missed Germany in a similar way I missed Israel. And I failed to see another point. Over the years, as I became rooted in California, I found that I missed Israel less, certainly not the way I had in my early years in America. For Hugo, it was probably the other way around. As things got tougher in Tel Aviv, he perhaps idealized certain moments from his childhood or from his career, and missing his Germany became stronger.

I go to the Kurhaus again, and suddenly I feel sorry for Hugo. It comes from nowhere, but as I think of Lucie and Hugo walking here back in 1925, holding the little girl's hands, my heart aches particularly for him, and for the first time, I feel a little closer to him. The garden café where my mother threw up the chocolate pudding is closed now. A homeless man is sitting under the awning looking at the rain. I look at the garden one more time, at the paths they walked back in 1925, and I say to myself that it's probably the last time in my life that I'll see it. I hold the glass door that leads to the garden, and after a moment, I close it behind me and pass the spectacular lobby.

After eating the soup, and the bread that came with it, I am not hungry, but I feel that this visit deserves a better ending. One item on the Kurhaus restaurant's menu catches my attention: *Oma's Himbeerteller* (Grandma's raspberry plate). Not something that my Oma ever served, but I need some comfort. A pianist plays a popular tune. At the table next to me, a dozen young people are having dinner. They are from all over the world, maybe a group of reps for a high-tech or pharmaceutical company. The plate comes with a huge number of berries and a dish of sugar, some whipped cream, and a sweet and sour sauce. Oma, someone's Oma, did not disappoint.

When I finish my dessert, I go to the garden to peek at it one more time. A young woman in white running clothes is jogging in the rain. The homeless guy is gone. Three young men dressed in grey and black are playing Pétanque.

"Yesss!" one of them shouts, in English, when his ball gets closest to the edge.

I can almost see Hugo, Lucie, and their little daughter walking on the path, and it's hard for me to leave them here.

22 DÜSSELDORF
"AND THEN WE'LL CONTINUE TO HAMM..."

After Yom Kippur, as if they couldn't stand the pampering that Wiesbaden offered, Lucie and Hugo decided to leave the spa town. It seemed that they were now determined to follow the pain axis: Hamm, Hannover, and maybe even beyond that. "In Düsseldorf, we'll say hi to the cartwheelers," Lucie wrote in a postcard to my sister and me, "and then we'll continue to Hamm, where *Ima'le* [Mommy] and Raphi were born." The postcard featured Düsseldorf's famous tradition of kids cartwheeling in joy. She sounded so cheerful that maybe when our mom read us this postcard, Eva and I imagined Oma and Opa cartwheeling all the way into Hamm.

Everything went smoothly in Düsseldorf. Lucie went shopping, Hugo wrote letters and rested in their room, and Dr. Panse continued to plan the psychiatric clinic in the city. It didn't matter that in 1940 he had sent mentally ill people to their deaths. It didn't matter that he had taught classes on "racial hygiene" during the Nazi time. Germany was looking forward to the future. Lucie was looking forward into the future. Dr. Panse was looking forward to the future, the same future in which they would meet.

Hugo was reserved and cautious regarding the visit: "There isn't much to see there, so we won't stay more than a day," he wrote in a letter to my mom. A longer stay in Hamm would cause "a shift in the atmosphere," he noted.

As far as I can tell, Hugo and Lucie didn't announce their plans to anyone in Hamm, except to one Jewish friend who would come from another town to meet them there. I assume that they also contacted Friedrich Kieserling, the lawyer who had helped Hugo with a claim for the loss of his profession. (Kieserling was also one of the local lawyers who had tried to help Hugo in 1933 by supporting his request for a good conduct certificate, which was needed to continue to appear in court but that was rejected.)[1]

I can't tell what Hugo planned or expected because he didn't write about it in his letters. But could he not toy, even for a moment, with the sweet dream of the exiled? For example, maybe he'd meet the president of the Higher Regional Court (*Oberlandesgericht*) who had informed him that he couldn't be a lawyer because he did not belong to the Aryan race. Or he'd meet one of his colleagues who had not spoken up against it, and after the first shock, that person would ask what he'd been up to lately, and later, with some hesitation, would gently ask, "Will Dr. Mendel consider the option of coming back?" They need people like him.

Ach! He's busy with other things, much more important things, he'd tell his former colleagues. They certainly have heard about the Jewish state, had they not? Yes, great things are happening there.

No. no. This doesn't ring true. It's not that he's busy, he will tell them, he actually has plenty of free time, but he will never set foot in a German court again. Once upon a time, he had had great respect for the German legal system. He remembers how proud he was, as a law student, when he had learned about the independence of the justice system from the state—that judges were subject to the law, and only to the law. That a citizen could have a dispute with the state and win. But not anymore. What a joke! He's sick to his stomach when he remembers how quickly the legal system crumbled under Hitler. And not much seems to have changed. Have the gentlemen seen the ridiculously short sentences that war criminals are receiving now?

Yes, this is what he'd tell them in Hamm.

23 HAMM

"I COULD HAVE SPENT SEVERAL MORE DAYS THERE."

I'm driving to Hamm with Dr. Paul Otto Samuelsdorff, the son of Dr. Erich Samuelsdorff who died here in 1954 while trying to reestablish his law firm. If the lawyers Hugo met in Frankfurt (Ernst Katzenstein and Manfred Herzfeld) represent a relatively optimistic ending to the story, Samuelsdorff senior represents a sad ending. I picked up Paul Otto from his apartment in Cologne. He is around 80 years old but looks great for his age—for any age—tan, fit, with solid grey hair. We speak Hebrew, which is one of 15 or so languages that he commands (including Swahili, which he learned and taught in Kenya). He's wearing a slightly oversized blazer, which gives him the look of a university professor, which he is. In 1956, after serving in both the British and the Israeli armies, Paul Otto returned to Germany from Tel Aviv. He studied linguistics and philosophy and became a professor of linguistics at the University of Cologne.[1]

When he opened the door, I said, "Shalom, Dr. Samuelsdorff."

"Call me Saul," he said in Hebrew with a slight German accent and shook my hand. I noticed how warm his hand was. When we went down to the street, I apologized that I'd come to pick him up in a fancy Mercedes. "I booked something smaller, but they upgraded me," I said, and he laughed.

We have several things in common, which we discover on the road: Neither of us is a big fan of George W. Bush or Ariel Sharon. Both of our fathers died on their birthdays.[2] And apparently, neither of us has a great sense of direction. On our way to Hamm, we want to visit Mechtild Brand, who has written a book about the Jews of Hamm and lives in Schwefe, a village 25 minutes out of town. I have a feeling we've been driving in circles for a while as we look for this elusive village.

Paul Otto (Saul) experienced a very similar childhood to my mom's. Before 1933, they didn't feel too different as Jews. He only remembers one incident of antisemitism in some vacation resort. On Sundays, the Jewish kids of Hamm had Hebrew school in a classroom by the synagogue, and this is where Paul Otto (who's a year younger than my mom) studied with her. Hugo was among the leaders of the local Jewish community, and in this capacity, he also took care of the synagogue. How this went with his tradition of eating grapes on the balcony on Yom Kippur isn't clear to me. I wonder whether Oma and Opa stopped on their visit to Hamm at the synagogue, which is now a parking lot. Mechtild will know (if we ever find her village). Maybe she also knows whom they met in Hamm and whether they visited the courthouse.

The court building of the *Oberlandesgericht* (Higher Regional Court) is another thing Paul Otto and I have in common. His father and my grandfather Hugo belonged to an exclusive club of lawyers that was authorized to appear in that court. In April 1933, the letter my grandfather received informing him that he could not appear in court named one Jewish lawyer who would still be allowed "for now" to appear. That lawyer was Dr. Erich Samuelsdorff, who had served as an officer in World War I. Paul Otto tells me that when they started to arrest Jews that month, his father set his army officer coat and the Iron Cross on a chair at the entrance. When they would come to get him, he would put on the coat and the iron cross and walk out to the street as a proud German officer. They didn't come.

"I think it may be the next village," Paul Otto says.

I'm optimistic.

They did come to arrest Hugo. Mirjam, who was 11 years old, asked her mother about the shouting at the entrance, and Lucie said these were some unhappy clients of Dad but that things will be all right. Lucie and Hugo did everything possible to shield their kids. When the furniture of the house was auctioned, they made sure the kids were away. When the family left Hamm, they made it feel like they were heading for a vacation in some resort town, which incidentally wasn't far from the truth. Lucie and the kids did leave for a small resort on the shore of Lake Lucerne in Switzerland, Weggis, where they waited for Hugo who went to southern Germany to purchase the machines for the factory. On their way to Palestine, they took the kids to Rome, Naples, and Athens. Vacation.

* * *

I'd met Mechtild once before when I had visited Hamm in 1994, a couple of years after my mother died. She picked me up from the train station, which looked the same in 1956, so I can imagine how my grandparents Lucie and Hugo arrived on the train from Düsseldorf, walking among all the passengers toward the exit of the building, maybe holding hands.

Paul Otto and I finally see the sign that announces the entrance to Schwefe. Mechtild opens the door with a warm smile. She has gray hair, pinkish cheeks, and a mix of integrity and sarcasm that reminds me of my mom. Paul Otto had met her several times when she was working on her book, and although I have met her only once, I've known her vicariously through my mom's letters. Their budding friendship was cut short by my mom's death three years after they had met, but they managed to squeeze in letters, phone calls, a visit to my sister Eva's Kibbutz in Israel, and a two-day trip to the former German Democratic Republic.

Mechtild has two cats that sometimes bring her presents from the neighboring fields in the shape of dead critters. "It's their way of contributing to the household budget," she says. We sit in her small and cozy living room, and she serves delicious plums she's picked from the public trees in the village and cookies that she's baked with her 7-year-old granddaughter.

"Your grandparents never visited Hamm," Mechtild says as if she were reading the questions on my mind. I'm surprised but not shocked. When I was going through the letters my grandparents had sent from the trip, I noticed the absence of a letter that describes their visit to Hamm. Maybe the letter was lost, I thought to myself. Or perhaps more likely, the visit was so painful that they waited until they were back in Israel to tell my mom about it in person. Now it turns out that they never even went.

"Everything is here in this folder," Mechtild tells me and opens a thick cardboard folder packed with documents, and after a few minutes of searching, pulls a letter from the folder and reads it to me. It's an affidavit by Dr. Goldstein from Düsseldorf who'd examined Hugo on September 19 and 20, 1956, and advised him not to go back to the city he had left 23 years earlier.

I look at the ugly brown cardboard folder, and it's clear to me that the story is getting complicated. When I told Mechtild that I was coming, she immediately informed me that she had a file here for me about Hugo, but I didn't think it was so big—dozens of letters and documents, it weighs at least four pounds. Looking at this folder makes me restless, like someone who signed up for a ten-mile race and then is told that he has to run another ten miles. I thought I would follow my grandparents' letters and that would be it, but now I'm beginning to think that the box of letters was just the beginning and that this brown folder will take me somewhere else. When I'm back in Menlo Park, I'll have to find Nadine and see whether she's willing to help me translate the new material.

It is clear to me that this folder holds many answers to my questions, and yet, it drives me nuts that I had to travel to a small village in Germany to find it. I have no one to blame for this but myself because this folder was born on my mother's typewriter in the room next to mine. As a child, I must have seen it a thousand times and probably dismissed it as just part of "my mom's work in German." As an adult, it turns out that my mom had offered to send me this folder, but I'd declined ("What will I do with a bunch of documents in German?" I must have thought to myself). And even after my mom had died, when my sister and I sorted her papers, we held this folder in our hands for a few seconds before we followed her written instructions to send it to Mechtild. Only later would I realize how lucky we were that Mechtild kept this folder because without it, I would not have known my mother's part in the story.

Mechtild will come to my hotel tomorrow to give me an overview of what's in the thick folder. She walks us outside, and I apologize for the fancy Mercedes that looks like an arrogant overgrown boy next to Mechtild's small car. I explain that I booked something smaller but that I got an upgrade, and Mechtild laughs and says she was wondering what I was doing with such a large car. Paul Otto and I drive to Hamm, which we find easily this time. Walking in the city, he draws my attention to a small swastika that someone had sketched with a marker on a wall. "They hate me. I hate them," he says. Despite his 80 years, I have some difficulties catching up with him. We go to see his family's house on Ostring Street. It's a large villa, and I think of the small apartment where his father had died after returning to Hamm. Paul Otto also shows me the house of another Jewish lawyer, Dr. Griesbach, who lived next door with his family. Once, non-Jewish kids told Paul Otto's brother that the Jews had killed Jesus. The boy thought for a moment and said, "I'm sure it's no one from our family. Maybe it's one of the Griesbachs."

The following day, Mechtild comes to my hotel, and we spend several hours reviewing some key documents in the thick folder. It's a claim related to Hugo that was handled by Dr. Lichtenstein, my mom's boss in Tel Aviv. Perhaps some dust awakened from the old file makes me sneeze, and Mechtild says in Hebrew: Labriut (bless you). She lived in Israel for a year as a volunteer in a village for adults with special needs, and she hosted enough Israelis in Hamm to pick up more than a few words in Hebrew.

Her relationships with the Jews of Hamm started in 1963 after she couldn't break through the wall of silence in her city: At first, the adults told her that there had been no Jews in Hamm, so there was no Jewish persecution. Then she was told that the city archive disappeared. Then someone referred her to the restitution authorities, but they didn't respond to her inquiries. She remembers how one time she came home completely confused after a day of futile research. One of her mom's friends who was still a fan of Hitler was visiting, and when she heard what Mechtild was researching, she started shouting at her that she was a traitor and a *Nestbeschmutzer* (fouling her own nest). Eventually, Mechtild found some addresses of local Jews around the world and started sending out letters, and this is how the first connections were established (not with my mom, who ignored Mechtild's letter at that point.)

Mechtild does everything she can to explain the legal matters to me, but after a while, I feel lost in the sea of documents.

"Some more letters by Dr. Lichtenstein..." I sigh, as I flip through more rustling pages.

"Yes, but I'm sure they were all written by your mother," Mechtild is quick to point out.

This should be said. My mom was way beyond what comes to mind when we think of a typical secretary in the 1960s. Yes, she took dictation and typed Dr. Lichtenstein's letters, but with every letter she typed, she learned something new. Erwin Lichtenstein found in my mom a thirsty student who in this way partially fulfilled her dream to study law. After a while, she engaged in fairly independent legal work. Dr. Lichtenstein was the one who signed the letters, but in many cases, she was the one who did the work.

A few documents later, we come across a decision of the court in Hugo's case that arrived at Lichtenstein's office when my mom was on vacation abroad. It is followed by a letter from Dr. Lichtenstein to Lucie, suggesting they wait with their response until my mom is back. Mechtild laughs.

"Just to show the role of your mother."

* * *

My mom resisted visiting Germany for the longest time. While Dr. Lichtenstein and his wife would regularly travel to Germany for work or vacation, my mom refused to go. I suspect that what had happened to her dad after his 1956 visit was a big reason for that. Another reason was that she did not have someone to go with. This changed after both Eva and I left home. When we were kids, no men were seen in our house, but now my mom had a partner, a good man by the name of Hertz Rappaport. In 1980 they decided to visit England together, and my mom spent the weeks before the trip getting over her fear of escalators (that originated in a dramatic fall after her first attempt to use these rolling steps). And after spending an afternoon at a department store in Tel Aviv, bravely leaping on this strange machine, she was ready. A year later, in 1981, they decided to go to Germany, and my mom spent the weeks before the trip building shields and armor around her. Indeed, the trip to Germany was uneventful. She reported that everything looked very nice, like in England, France, or Italy. She told me that it was surreal to arrive at the train station in Hamm and walk home from there, just as she had as a kid. But she didn't allow it to get to her. Only when she stood in front of the courthouse in Munich, where Hugo had appeared several times, the rage caught her. She was happy to leave Germany.

At the time, she didn't know Mechtild, and after that visit, she had no intention of ever going back. A few years later, Mechtild visited Israel, and this is when they met for the first time and started corresponding. When my mom got an invitation from the city of Hamm to participate in a gathering of former Jewish residents, she preferred to stay home. But the following year another invitation arrived, and Mechtild nudged her to go. My mom respected Mechtild not only for her research into the past but also for her efforts to promote tolerance in the present. So in 1991, my mom and my sister, Eva, went to Hamm for that gathering. Mechtild tells me about that visit of my mom's in Hamm when she suddenly stops.

"Your mother arrived in Hamm exactly a year before she died," she says. "She died on September 20, 1992, and she came to Hamm on September 20, 1991."

I think of the fact that my mom remembered the death anniversaries of everyone in the family—except for that of her grandmother Nettchen Stern because nobody knows where and when exactly she died. And I think of the fact that my mom arrived in Hamm at her minus one *yahrzeit*,[3] which she didn't know either because nobody knows when he or she will die (except for those who kill themselves). On that visit, my mom went with Mechtild and Eva to East Germany, and when they were back, they participated in the gathering where they met Paul Otto and other acquaintances.

But it seems to me that the most meaningful day occurred a day before the big meeting. In the morning, a young man from a volunteer group in Hamm drove her ("in his mom's Fiesta" my mom noted) to the city of Münster , 28 miles north of Hamm, where the state archive holds the personal files of the local Jewish lawyers. "Opa's file was already waiting," she wrote to me. (This was not the file that Mechtild gave me but a file that documents Hugo's legal career). For several hours she read, took notes, and made copies from three volumes of all his certificates and diplomas covering years of study and practice: matriculation tests, university records, bar exams, internship records from courts and law offices. "I could have spent several more days there," she wrote, but she didn't want the guy with his mom's Fiesta to wait for too long. There was no immediate reason for her to sit in that archive. The legal case involving her father had been settled for years; Mechtild's book had already been published. My mom simply wanted to be with her dad.

Before she leaves the hotel, Mechtild asks whether I'd like to see where my grandfather's law office was. I saw it on my 1994 visit, but I want to see it again now that I know about the bond that was formed there between a father and a daughter. It's a five-minute walk from the hotel, at the address I know from the green envelopes in Oma's apartment: "Dr. jur. Mendel | Rechtsanwalt u. Notar | Hamm (Westf.) | Große Weststraße 24 [1.] | Fernsprecher 967".[4] The street is now a pedestrian mall, and there's a butcher shop on the ground floor of number 24. I look up at the second floor of the red brick building. Here is where the four-year-old typist learned her ABCs. Here, when she was ten, he taught her paragraphs from the German Civil Code. This is where the pact between them was formed. This is where they decided that one day they'd form a partnership, never imagining how things would unfold.[5]

24 MENDEN
"WE DIDN'T IDENTIFY ANYTHING."

In January 1946, an American military jeep approached the crossing point between the American occupied zone and the British occupied zone in Germany. The MP raised his arm to stop the two soldiers in the jeep, in case they hadn't noticed the gate, the barbed wire, and the signs. After the war, Germany was divided into four zones—American, British, Soviet, and French—and crossing between zones was highly restricted. Europe was agitated enough after six years of war, and the signs all around made it clear that the no-crossing rules were strictly enforced.

The soldier sitting next to the driver, a young private first class who looked like a kid, handed the MP a letter from his mom, or more precisely, a letter from General Dwight D. Eisenhower who had gotten a letter from the soldier's mom. In her letter, the soldier's mother asked the Commanding General of the US forces in Europe to give her son special permission to visit her parents (his grandparents) in Menden, which was in the British occupied zone. A few months earlier, her parents had been released from the concentration camp Theresienstadt after spending three years there, and they were now back home. "Since he is in Europe at the present time, I thought it would be nice for him to visit his grandparents," the soldier's mom wrote. "It might be the last opportunity to see them." The MP stepped into the guardhouse to make a phone call, and came out after a couple of minutes and made a sign to his colleague who raised the gate. The American Jeep crossed into the British zone.

Almost 60 years later, Mechtild Brand and I are in the car on our way to Menden. As opposed to Hamm, which they avoided on the doctor's order, there is no sign in their letters that they'd even planned to visit Menden. The only time that Hugo referred to that region was after he'd tried to identify Menden on the flight from Munich to Amsterdam and reported flatly, "We didn't identify anything," which made me want to visit even more. Perhaps I'll learn something about a man who isn't curious about the place where he had grown up. I was happy when Mechtild offered to join me, although I'm not sure why she did. Maybe out of some sense of responsibility for a son of a former resident of Hamm with a compromised sense of direction. I like her stories. Her cats brought three presents last night: two dead mice and one that was still alive, at least when it was brought in.

A little meadow that we pass reminds Mechtild of something my mom had told her. Oma and Opa used to take little Mirjam out to the meadow to play, but she would insist on bringing a book along, and she would sit and read it. They wanted her to run in the grass and explore nature, but she wanted her books. I had never heard this story, but it rings true: My mother was happiest when she had "a printed word in front of her nose," as she used to say. And it's true that her parents (especially Lucie) wanted her to be tougher. One day (and this is a story I heard a million times) Lucie saw three boys pushing a soapbox car in Hamm, and she nudged Mirjam to ask them for a ride. The little girl had no interest, so Lucie asked the kids directly, and when they saw the girl's scared face, they were happy to help. "Slowly!" the girl pleaded with them as the metal wheels started skipping on the cobbled street. Is there a stronger catalyst for three boys who push a cart than a girl who begs them to slow down? My mom never forgot that ride.

In Menden, Mechtild and I meet Franz Rose, a local historian who has written a book about the Jews of the town. He is about 70 years old, balding, wearing glasses, and carrying a black briefcase with several copies of his book. Before he retired, he was a salesman, and he is a passionate collector not only of facts but also of fossils, rocks, and ancient stone tools. As a child, he remembers the American soldier's visit. Franz was around 15, and even though almost 60 years have passed, he remembers very well the chocolate the soldier who had looked like a kid gave him. He also remembers his father telling him that in 1938 after Ernst Mendel was released from his arrest by the Gestapo, his hand was in a large bandage. Franz's father asked Ernst what had happened, and Ernst didn't want to say. Mechtild says that when people were released from arrest, they had to sign a form vowing to keep quiet about what had happened to them. Franz takes us to *Synagogengasse* (the synagogue alley). He says that when the synagogue was set on fire, the neighbors were quick to put it out. I'm touched by the courage of ordinary Germans who stood up to bullies, but then Franz says that they did it because they were concerned that the fire would spread to their houses.

My grandfather Hugo was born in Unna, about ten miles away, to his mother, Emilie, and his father, Emanuel, a teacher who also gave sermons at local synagogues. Hugo was a weak child, and when he was two years old, his stronger brother, Ernst, was born. Two years later, a sister was born—Liese (the famous Tante Liese). On their vacations, they would visit their grandma Bella Samson, who was managing the family's store in Menden, which offered endless adventures to the kids. On the first floor, you could look at the rolls of colorful fabric or touch the silk ties and the buckskin trousers. A few steps up, you could peek at the women from the surrounding farms as they would be trying on the latest fashions from Berlin. In the second building, under the sign *Samsons Bettenlager*, where sheets and blankets would be sold, you could chase a goose feather that had escaped from a down duvet or watch the huge drum turning where blankets would be refreshed. And when Grandma Bella wasn't around (and only when she wasn't around), you could slide through the long corridor on the second floor.

In 1904, when Hugo was 13, the world he had known crashed overnight. His mother, Emilie, died after an illness, and his father, Emanuel, seemed to be unable to take care of the three kids on his own. The store in Menden, which used to be an adventure, now became their new home, and not a regular home. Bella was almost 70 years old, and maybe the death of her daughter added to her toughness. Her son and second-in-command, Max, boosted the house's craziness.

Max had no kids of his own. He lived next door to the store with his petite housekeeper, Frau Brinkschulte, who had a room in the attic (at least this is how Martin remembered it). Officially, Max Samson was Jewish, and his name appears in the list of the small synagogue of Menden, but it doesn't seem that he was a frequent prayer. In contrast, Martin remembered the pork legs that were hanging in Max's attic to dry. An avid hunter, he would walk on the weekends into the forest, a green Alpine hat on his head, with his long barrel gun and his beloved dog, Wolf, running ahead. He liked the open air, and the windows in his house had to be kept open too. In the cold mornings, Frau Brinkschulte could be seen hanging the duvet of Master Samson over the window, her teeth chattering. Even though I never met the guy, his name invokes a sense of fear in me as I remember the expression on my mom's face when she would talk about Onkel Max, who had a bad temper and a short fuse. He loved scaring her with stories about witches or gypsies who kidnap kids and hide them in the forest. He also liked to drink, and his rage attacks were remembered by the family years after he'd died. When the three Mendel kids moved to Menden, Ernst and Hugo had a new challenge: to protect each other and their little sister, Liese, from Onkel Max. Hugo was the "lawyer," and Ernst was the strong one.

When Hugo graduated from high school, it seems that he wanted to get as far away as possible from Menden. From Onkel Max, from the smallness of Menden, but maybe most important, from being a merchant, which was his most likely destiny there. He wanted more. Liese also left Menden the moment she could, and only Ernst stayed, and married Else, the daughter of Sally and Malchen Leven, who owned a shoe store in town. By then, grandmother Bella was no longer alive. Max, who didn't like the match, was in constant conflict with Else and with Ernst, his second-in-command at the store. Ernst was the head of the athletic club in Menden, and Max was the hunter. The conflict between them did not involve guns, but fistfights were not unheard of.

Franz takes us to the Jewish cemetery. Both Bella and Max died before the war—Bella in 1918 and her son Max in 1937, possibly the last person to be buried here. Franz points his finger to a door hidden in the dense vegetation and explains that it leads to a bomb shelter dug under the cemetery. Perhaps the people of Menden felt that the safest place to hide from the Allies' bombs was under Bella and Max Samson and the rest of their dead Jewish neighbors.

* * *

The American soldier and his driver parked their Jeep in the plaza in front of city hall in Menden, when the soldier heard someone calling his name in a Westphalian accent he had not heard in eight years:

"Martin Mendel!"

It was Martin's friend from elementary school, Walter Kordier, who was half Jewish and had spent part of the war in a forced labor camp. From here, Martin rushed to his grandparents' house. The shop window of the shoe store on the ground floor was covered with wood planks. Upstairs, Martin found his mom's parents, Sally and Malchen Leven. They had changed in the past eight years (three of them in a camp), but they certainly were not the emaciated survivors Martin had seen crawling in the snow in Dachau a few months earlier. His grandmother Malchen had grown up in the countryside and knew how to identify mushrooms and other edible plants. For a while, she'd also worked in the camp's kitchen.

There were also acts of true kindness in Menden. When things turned bad before and during the war, their Catholic neighbors, the Stracke family, would leave food on the steps of the Mendels and the Levens after dark. Else or Malchen would bring it in after a while. Now Martin and his grandparents paid a visit to the Strackes and brought some canned food and dried fish that Martin had stuffed in his jeep. And as they were all sitting in the living room, enjoying American chocolate, somebody suggested that the young folks do something that they used to do as kids. And Martin and the two Stracke girls who were about his age put their roller skates on and skated around town like in the old days. And I imagine the three of them, an American kid in uniform and two German girls, gliding along the streets of Menden, and Eddie the blue jay circling above.

Then Martin went to see the Samsons' store, which looked like a dusty, empty tuna can, years after its content had been consumed. The sign *Samsons Bettenlager* was faded but still legible, and Martin found a cardboard sign that Ernst had made just before they left, announcing the sale of fabric leftovers. Franz takes Mechtild and me to see the street corner where the store used to be, and it strikes me how indifferent I am. The building is nice and clean, but I feel no connection to it. Martin told me once that he immediately feels creepy when he's in Menden. Franz always tells him how he belongs to "good old Menden," but Martin said he didn't feel part of it. I know what he meant. I feel more connected to Hamm, maybe because I have been there before, and my mom and Eva were there, maybe because of Mechtild and Paul Otto. There's something distant in Menden, perhaps because it's linked in my mind only with Hugo. My mom hardly ever mentioned the place, and it seems to me that even for Hugo, Menden was mostly associated with Onkel Max and not with fond memories that the young boy Hugo had here. But there's another thing, and maybe this is the real reason Hugo stayed away from Menden. As a teenager, all he wanted was to break away from the life of a merchant who sells fabric or bedding. As a young man, he managed to leave Menden and be the first in his family to study at a university and become a lawyer with the title "Dr." preceding his name. Yet in the last two decades of his life, he was reluctantly dragged back. After all the years of studying, exams, and internships, he was a merchant again, and not even a store owner, but one who peddles his wares from one merchant to another in the heat of Tel Aviv, knowing that Menden got him after all.[1]

25 NORTHEIM
"ONE DID NOT KNOW."

I arrive at the train station in Northeim in the afternoon. The young woman at the taxi stand says that all the cabs are away and it would take at least ten or 15 minutes before a cab would be at the station. I decide to walk. It's a beautiful day, and although I've never been here, I know the general direction. *Bahnhofstraße* (the train station street) leads to the town square, and on the other side of the square is *Breite Straße* (the wide street) where Oma was born in 1898. When I arrive at *Breite Straße* after a ten-minute walk, the bouncing sound of my suitcase's wheels on the cobblestones announces: Lucie's back in town. Lucie's back in town. Lucie's back in town.

I stop at house number 14. There's a shoe shop where Oma's parents had once had their clothing store. They had lived above the store, and I'm pretty sure that Hugo and Lucie were married in the backyard. It seems to me that Lucie's parents, Louis and Nettchen Stern, were happy with the young lawyer who was marrying their daughter. There was probably some friction around religious issues though. Nettchen kept a kosher kitchen, and Hugo came from a less strict background (maybe Lucie told her parents about pork hanging in Onkel Max's attic). Lucie ate everything in restaurants, but she wanted her parents to be able to visit the young family in Hamm. So a compromise was reached: Lucie would keep a kosher kitchen, and Hugo would confine his consumption of *Speck* (bacon) to something they called the *Treif Ecke* (the non-kosher corner), which was a wooden cutting board they dedicated to this purpose.

My hotel is a few doors down the street from the house, and I go to my room there to take a nap. Later, when I leave the hotel for a walk, it's already dark, and I'm struck by thousands of small lights that decorate the street for Christmas. Hidden loudspeakers play holiday songs in English: "Chestnuts roasting on an open fire." Oma's street turns into an outdoor shopping mall before Christmas, with little decorated huts selling wooden toys, wool hats, warm wine, glazed apples, and roasted chestnuts. In front of Oma's house, there's a small coin-operated helicopter that is moving up and down with a happy kid inside (at least he seems happy). A few houses down, there's a bookstore named Spannaus. The name sounds familiar as I walk in, but for the life of me, I can't remember from where. Maybe it's part of a chain I saw in another German city. I browse for a while and leave. It's cold, and "Santa Claus Is Comin' to Town" is now playing.

I buy a bag of roasted almonds and walk around the festive square, and suddenly it occurs to me why the name Spannaus is so familiar. In researching the history of Northeim, I read a book by an American historian named William Sheridan Allen, who studied the rise of Nazism in Germany. To do this, he chose to put one town under his microscope, and in the first edition of the book (published in 1965), he concealed the identity of the city. In the following year, however, the German magazine *Der Spiegel* exposed the name of the city: it was Northeim. When Allen published a revised edition in 1984, he used the real name of the city and also revealed some names of the people involved. One of these people was Wilhelm Spannaus, the owner of the bookstore, who according to Allen, was one of the first people in Northeim to join the Nazi Party and played an important role in legitimizing it. He was well liked in town and an intellectual, and as one Northeimer told Allen, once Wilhelm Spannaus joined the party, people said, "If he's in it, it must be all right."[1]

In the morning, I walk around town and come across another bookstore. Some *Harry Potter* books in the window invite me in. Behind the counter, a friendly woman with a round face smiles and asks whether she could help me. I ask if she has any books about the history of Northeim, and we strike up a conversation. I tell her that my grandmother was born here, and she says she knows some old-timers and that she can ask if they remember her. After my experience in Wiesbaden, I carry some photos with me, and I give her a picture of Lucie with some of her classmates. I also give her a picture of Nettchen, Lucie's mom, who was the last person from the family to leave Northeim. I tell her that they were Jewish, but I think she'd already guessed that. She promises to check. You never know.

Nettchen's story haunted Oma all of her adult life, and it didn't surprise me that Northeim wasn't even mentioned in their letters. No, Lucie and Hugo did not visit Northeim on their 1956 trip. Since Hamm, I no longer follow them, but rather their sorrow. Soon I'll rejoin them, but in the meantime, I'm making a detour to visit their cities of pain. I never spoke with Oma about it, but in the few times that I'd discussed this with my mother, she just said, *"One did not know. One did not know."* (She said it twice, emphasizing every word). As a teenager, I likely didn't fully comprehend what she said. Like that Israeli girl who asked during the Eichmann trial why the Israeli army had not helped the Jews in the camps, somewhere in my head I was asking myself, *What do you mean, "One did not know"?* Hadn't she heard about the Holocaust?

In 1935, when Lucie and Hugo already lived in Tel Aviv, Nettchen came to stay with them (Louis had died in 1924). It isn't clear if she came just for a visit or to permanently move to Tel Aviv. Little is remembered in the family from this trip. In my hotel room, I look through my papers and notes. Raphi had told me about Nettchen's visit to Tel Aviv, but he wasn't sure about the dates. My mom's cousin Ruth had told me it was in 1935–1936, but I didn't have anything to document it. As if to add some hesitation to the story, in the only picture from Tel Aviv, Nettchen's face was touched so many times by a grieving hand that it can no longer be recognized. But while I'm not sure about the exact dates, I am sure that she returned to Germany, and I know that she was sent by the Nazis to Riga on December 15, 1941, because I found her name in the transport list to that city.

I walk to City Hall, across the river, where I have an appointment with the mayor of Northeim and the city archivist. The mayor, Irnfried Rabe, a little balding with gray hair, is warm and welcoming. So is the city archivist, Ekkehard Just, who is younger, with a mustache and dark hair. Mr. Just pulls out a copy of the family record and hands it to me. A big J is stamped on the upper left corner of the card, and the mayor, just in case I missed it, draws my attention to it. My uncertainty about the dates of Nettchen's visit to Palestine disappear. On December 2, 1935, Nettchen left Northeim. Under "destination," I see Tel Aviv and the exact address of Lucie and Hugo at the time: 60 *Chovevei Zion* Street, which was a bigger apartment, one where they had lived before losing their money. The next lines on the card are the painful ones: on March 26, 1936, after about three months in Tel Aviv, Nettchen returned to *Breite Straße* 14. Finally, on November 2, 1938, she left for Hannover.[2]

And here we come to the silences that I suspect fell between Lucie and Hugo whenever Northeim was mentioned. Beyond my mother's "One did not know," I heard several explanations and splinters of answers to the question of why Nettchen left Tel Aviv to return to Nazi Germany. One explanation was that in 1936, her daughter, Käthe, (Lucie's sister) was still living in Germany with her family. The second explanation was that Hugo was not an easy person, and this did not help his relationship with his mother-in-law. What exactly happened, if it happened, I do not know. But maybe Hugo said something, or grumbled, or even just puffed impatiently. After all, we all know that sometimes there are small tensions with a guest and that sometimes things are said (even when the host is usually laid-back and even if the guest is there for a few days rather than a few months). And this is another cruel aspect of the Holocaust: that something you told your mother-in-law in the heat of the moment could start a chain of events that would lead to her death. I have no evidence that Hugo said anything that caused Nettchen to leave Tel Aviv, but I have a feeling that something happened and that this "something" was always there between Lucie and Hugo.

I show the two men—the mayor and the archivist—a yellowing newspaper clip that Lucie had kept all these years. It's a picture of a reunion with a woman named Marie Willerding; she had been both Lucie and Käthe's high school principal. They both laugh the way people laugh when they meet an old acquaintance. As it turns out, Ms. Willerding was a famous character in town, and for years, citizens have requested that a street be named after her, but no street was found.

"You can't just change a street name on people," Mr. Just says.

Recently, however, new sections of town have been developed, and finally, the city has named a street after the principal. Mr. Just tells me that her employment contract with the city from 1913 stated that she would need to quit her job if she ever got married. This did not come up. The mayor tells me how one of the older people who was photographed with the principal in the news clip used to take him aside whenever they would meet and try to convince him that Germany should capture the land it had lost in the war. When Mr. Rabe would tell him that there's no need for that, the man used to give him a "you're not a good German" look.

The mayor asks me if now, after 9/11, there's more control over the movement of citizens in America. He's not too optimistic about racism. "You can't stop this hatred," he says. "It's something that people have in their bones. You can just remind them, again and again, that there is another way so that the hatred is kept on the back burner." He sees this type of hatred against the Turkish population.

If anyone of the old-timers of Northeim recognized Lucie or Nettchen in the pictures that I gave the nice bookseller, they didn't contact me. But a few years later, a history teacher from Northeim by the name of Hans Harer wrote about Nettchen in the local newspaper.[3] His article didn't result in anyone from Northeim contacting me either. Except for one former Northeimer. That newspaper article by Hans Harer was forwarded by someone to Lotte Seidel (née Oppenheim) in a retirement home in Haifa, Israel, who had grown up in Northeim and remembered Nettchen very well. Lotte and her twin sister were nine years old when one day their mother took them to visit Nettchen Stern, who had just returned from Palestine. Lotte Seidel remembered two things that Nettchen had told them about the holy land: one was about the Yemenite Jewish women who were squatting on the floor, washing clothes by hand. The other thing was the fast sunset in Tel Aviv as opposed to the long, slow dusk in Germany.

Mrs. Seidel was somewhat reserved when I talked to her. She spoke slowly and tried to be precise. She told me about life as a child in Northeim, but she was not generous with her words. She emphasized that her family was more religious than some other families were and that they kept to themselves. She spent most of her time with her twin sister and not much with other kids. Suddenly though I sensed some excitement on the other end of the phone line. Something she said, or something I said, brought back a memory that had not surfaced for decades.

"I remember that one time, a girl from Hamm visited Nettchen Stern. Suddenly I remember that. She had large eyes, black hair. She was small and beautiful."[4]

When Nettchen returned from Palestine in 1936, several dozen Jews were still in Northeim, and Nettchen would go for long walks on Sundays with Frau Guttentag who managed the family store. But in January 1937, Frau Guttentag announced a sale of the store's contents, and in April, she came to say good-bye and return the key. In the same year, many other Jews left Northeim, and by September 1938, there were fewer than fifteen Jews in town. It seems that loneliness in the big city of Hannover looked more appealing to Nettchen than loneliness in Northeim did. On November 2, 1938, when she left her home, I assume that she rented a wagon or a car to take her trunk and suitcases from *Breite Straße* via *Bahnhofstraße* to the train station. Something in me refuses to believe that nobody snuck to the house to say good-bye, to say that they hope that things would get better soon. Grete Neuhaus, a Jewish neighbor from Northeim, wrote in a letter to Lucie in 1962 that Annie Böhme from Northeim had been good to Grete's family before they'd left for New York. I don't know whether Nettchen was that lucky.

26 HANNOVER

"I KNOW THAT IT SNOWED THAT DAY."

A week after Nettchen arrived in Hannover, the synagogue in town was burned down, but the letters that she sent to her daughters in Tel Aviv during the next few months were somewhat reassuring. She'd bought a nice bed and a dresser, and everyone says that her room is *gemütlich* (cozy). She is busy knitting a sweater for Ruth (my mom's cousin, who was now also in Tel Aviv), and she hopes to finish by Ruth's birthday. In another letter, she was less cheerful. Her neighbors kept the story from her for two weeks so that she wouldn't get upset. ("But I'm getting upset now," Nettchen noted.) Her Jewish neighbor, Erna Waller, decided to put an end to the depressing situation. She wrote letters to her friend, Mrs. Jacobs, to the doorman, and the cleaning lady and then dropped these letters in their mailboxes. Then she closed the windows, turned on the gas, and sat at the kitchen table. When Mrs. Jacobs got the letter, she rushed to the apartment and found Mrs. Waller dead. "She could not have done it differently," Nettchen wrote.[1]

With the beginning of the war, the letters from Nettchen stopped. In Tel Aviv, Lucie was in agony. How did she let her mom go back into the trap? Together with her sister, Käthe, she sent a letter through the Red Cross. They counted every word, so they ended picking the most trivial ones: "Dear Mom, we hope that you are healthy, like us. We haven't heard from you for a long time. Warm regards on your 70th birthday. Respond quickly, kiss, Käthe, Lucie." After a few weeks, they received a reassuring response, and after some time they sent another letter through the Red Cross where they managed to squeeze in what each of her grandkids was doing: "Hermann works here, Mirjam at a law office, Ruth studies housekeeping in Tel Aviv, Ludwig, a student." They received a letter back after a while in which Nettchen thanked them and added, "I miss you so much." This was the last time they ever heard from her.

* * *

I go to Ahlem, which used to be an agricultural school and served as a collection point for Jews who were deported to the East. It's still a school of some sort. When I arrive, some students notice me and ask whether they can help. One of them takes me to the school's office and announces joyfully:

"We have a guest from California!"

The secretary calls a man with a huge set of keys who takes me across the yard and opens a metal door for me. I walk downstairs into the basement that was used by the Gestapo to jail Jews and political rivals. It's now a small museum, and panels on the walls feature the names of the people who had gone through this place— Nettchen Stern among them. Later in the morning, a woman named Martina Mussmann, who works for the region's museums, comes to show me around. She tells me how in December 1941, the Nazis brought the Jews to Ahlem by trucks before putting them on trains to the East. We stand by the gates through which the trucks passed. Oma's mom was on one of those trucks.

"Do you know how cold it was?" I ask.

"I know that it snowed that day," Mrs. Mussmann says.[2]

Lucie and Hugo planned to go to Hannover too, but this plan fell through. Hugo wrote to my mom that Hermann Kugelmann, another Jewish lawyer they'd met in Wiesbaden, would take care of whatever had to be taken care of there. I take the train to the train station in Linden Hannover. Nettchen was brought there from Ahlem by a truck on December 15, 1941. The only other person who gets off the train with me is a young man wearing leather pants. Every spot in the station is covered with graffiti. A man and a woman, holding a young girl between them, cross the tracks running to board the train. The guy in leather pants shouts something after them. Maybe that they shouldn't do it. He walks into a graffiti-covered passage, and I follow him. Outside the station, I see him talking excitingly with two police officers in a light green uniform. Maybe he's telling them how upset he got at the people who'd crossed the tracks.

So here it all happened. I talked to two women who were on the same train as Nettchen was: Ruth Joffe from Arizona and Lore Oppenheimer from New York. They both were young girls, and there were 1001 people on the train that day, so I wasn't surprised that they didn't remember a 70-year-old woman. But they both remembered the conditions. I had imagined it as a cattle train, but Lore Oppenheimer told me it was a passenger train. Before the Jews boarded it, the Germans took everything away, but you could take things like sewing machines that were put in the last car. The doors were locked. You couldn't get out for three days. Nobody knew where the train was headed until a rumor spread that the final destination was Riga, Latvia.

27 RIGA

"WHAT A WONDERFUL WORLD."

Lore Oppenheimer told me that some older people were taken aside after getting off the train in Riga and were shot. Ruth Joffe said that it was freezing cold. Nobody knows for sure what happened to Nettchen in Riga. Her name appears on the list of those transported, so it's clear she was on that train, but that passenger list is the last official record we have of her.[1]

There is a Matisse exhibit in Riga this month, and the city is covered with posters announcing it. Riga is a beautiful city, but only here do I understand what Lucie wrote in one of her letters from Düsseldorf—that she could not enjoy this beauty. I take a cab to a section of town where the ghetto used to be. Maybe Nettchen died here. After the war, Lucie and Käthe received a letter from Erwin Mosbach, a son of one of their many cousins, who was deported to Riga too, survived the war, and ended up in Sweden. He wrote that Nettchen gave her food to young people and consequently died of starvation. It suddenly occurs to me that my mom and my grandma never traveled here and that maybe they would like me to do something on their behalf, so I pick a flower and leave it at the corner of a park in the ghetto.

I take a taxi to the mass graves outside of the city. If Nettchen wasn't shot at the train station or died in the ghetto, then she died here. It's a forest, and I'm all by myself. The taxi driver who drove me here offered to wait, but I told him to go, which I'm starting to regret. I notice some needles by a bench and some empty beer bottles, and I see a couple of people in the far distance, shouting and laughing. A woodpecker of some sort is making a pleasant noise. The soft wind goes through the trees, and some leaves fall on the ground. It's very quiet, and only the traffic from the main road can be heard from time to time. The mass graves are essentially just large cement frames of some raised dirt. My mother used to say, "What a wonderful world," when she would hear something on the news like a massacre of Blacks in South Africa or if she saw a picture of a burnt-down village in Vietnam. This is the first place on my trip where I break down and cry.

For many years after the war, my mom would regularly scan through the official publication of the Search Bureau for Missing Relatives, which listed survivors. Although it was clear that Nettchen had died, my mom never fully accepted her grandmother's death. I walk back to the main road. A taxi picks me up after a long time. Two miles later, the driver points out to a young woman standing by the road. "Fuck for money," he says and laughs and makes a gesture with his hand in case I'd missed his point. I manage to see her very pretty face as the cab speeds up to return to downtown Riga.

* * *

Raphi told me that when they would come to visit as kids, Nettchen would bless each grandchild. She would put her hands over their foreheads to say a blessing that had some mystical words in Hebrew that they did not understand. It was called *Benchen*, and it was part of the ritual of visiting Northeim.

On the corner of Reines Street and Dizengoff Square in Tel Aviv stood a metal electricity pole with a solid cement base, and an old one-legged beggar was always there, supporting himself by his crutches, half sitting on the cement. When we would pass by him, Oma would give me a coin, and I would approach him slowly, eyeing the empty part of his pants that was neatly folded above his knee. After I would give him the coin, he would put his hands on my head, close his eyes, and bless me. This was the only chance I had to see the face of an unshaved man from such a close distance, and I would peek at his bristles as he would say something I never understood about Abraham, Isaac, and Jacob. And when he would be done, I would sneak out from under his hands and run back to her, and Oma would nod at him, and we would continue our adventures on the streets of Tel Aviv.

28 DÜSSELDORF

"NICHT AHIN. NICHT AHER."

Lucie and Hugo stayed in Düsseldorf all this time, and this is where I rejoin them after the detour I'd taken to the cities of their pain. Now that we're together again, I decided to go to a variety show they had attended at the Apollo Theater. Oma was into this stuff—jugglers, clowns, magicians, and acrobats—and as a kid, I loved it when she would take me to such performances in Tel Aviv. (I remember her getting excited, at least as much as I was, to see a Chinese plate spinner.) As an adult, however, I have to admit that I'm less excited about such shows, especially not about acrobats who swing near the ceiling of a hall and might smash to the ground at any moment. Apollo is not a place you go to by yourself, and I feel more than a little awkward among the many couples and small groups that eat and drink around me. The cabaret décor with its red walls and chairs also contributes to my sense of alienation. Earlier today, the Apollo had an open house during which time the audience could go behind the scenes, and as I walked around, upstairs and downstairs, I found that I was mostly occupied by what has become an annoying habit of mine: finding places where Hugo had perhaps been considering jumping from. Only later will I find that the Apollo is now in a different building than the one they'd attended.

Falling is a recurring nightmare of mine. In my dreams, I'm not the one who falls, but other people fall from rooftops, balconies, or cliffs. Among the books that Oma would read us in German, there was one called *Struwwelpeter,* which famously chronicled the consequences of kids' bad deeds. If you play with matches, you'll catch fire; if you refuse to eat, you'll shrink and die, and if you suck your thumb, a big man with huge scissors will cut your thumb off. (Educational stuff written by a psychiatrist named Heinrich Hoffmann in 1845.) Among the many unfortunate kids in this book, there was one character, *Hans Guck-in-die-Luft* (Hans Look-in-the-air) who falls off a wharf because he always looks up instead of where he's going. I don't remember being that impressed by this story (the girl running with her dress burning left a much bigger impression on me), but maybe this is where my fear of falling started. Or maybe it only started after I learned about Hugo's suicide.

The Mendels were here with the Pincoffs to see the new comedy *Das Sonntagskind* with Heinz Rühmann, but before the movie started, there was a performance of acrobats. The traditional gong was heard, and people started flying in the air, as they now do in front of me. "Okay, okay, I get the idea," I say to myself, "Guys, this won't end well." There is a moment in almost any acrobatic trick when the acrobat is not here and not there. He releases his grip from one swing, hoping that the other swing will be waiting for him where he expects it. He jumps off the shoulders of one teammate, hoping to land on the shoulders of another. As they say in Yiddish *nicht ahin. Nicht aher* (Neither here nor there).

When my mom told me about Hugo's suicide, that evening at our home near Berkeley after dinner when the kids were asleep, she told me that this is what this trip did to him. He never felt that he belonged in Israel, and this trip made it clear to him that he did not belong in Germany either. He was in midair. Neither here nor there.

29 "DÜSSELDORF ISN'T WHAT IT USED TO BE."

Another man. Another city. Another staircase. The man is Primo Levi. The city is Turin, Italy. The staircase is the one at his apartment building. One day in 1987, the concierge knocked on the door of the famous author's apartment on the fourth floor to give him the mail. Mr. Levi took the envelopes and thanked her with a smile. A few minutes later, there was a terrible thump, and the man was found dead at the bottom of the stairs. And with that, a great debate arose, in fact, two debates that continue to this day. The first: did he fall, or did he jump? The second: If he jumped, why did he jump? Was it related to what had happened to him in Auschwitz, or was it caused by a depression that has a physiological explanation: perhaps a side effect of a drug or an operation from which he was recovering?[1]

The following day Lucie went to Graf-Adolf Strasse to do some shopping, and Hugo stayed in the room to write a letter to his daughter. Life is a bit easier here because they know more people than in Wiesbaden. Yesterday they met a couple from Israel who are on their way to Canada. I'm amazed by how many Jewish acquaintances they had in Germany. Most of them were on their way to somewhere—the United States, Canada, or Australia—"Or at least this is what they say," Hugo wrote. He added that most of them also talked very positively about Israel. Only one Jewish couple they knew explained that they left Israel because "there are too many Jews there."[2]

The postcard they sent that week featured Düsseldorf's famous "Fountain of Youth": three naked kids sit on a rock looking at three frogs that spray delicate streams of water into a pool. Or maybe it's three frogs that look at three naked kids. One can argue about this too. And as streams of coffee were poured into china cups at the houses where Hugo and Lucie were visiting, two arguments about Hugo Mendel's future death were starting to materialize. The first argument: did he fall or did he jump? The second argument: If he jumped, why did he jump? Was it related to what had happened to him, or was it caused by a depression that had a physiological explanation?

Here in Düsseldorf, Dr. Panse (the director of the psychiatric clinic) categorically rejected any traumatic aftereffects of external psychological stressors and kept searching for physiological explanations for psychological difficulties. Of course, the fact that he had been a member of the Nazi Party doesn't mean that *everything* he believed in was wrong. Clearly, there are physiological drivers of depression and familial ones. (Those whose grandfathers committed suicide, like Primo Levi or me, are more likely to commit suicide themselves.)

What is outrageous in Panse's view is the *categorical* rejection of external stressors. As if anyone can unequivocally tell that what Primo Levi had been through in Auschwitz had nothing to do with his depression and that it can all be explained by chemical reactions or genetic matter. As if Mrs. Waller, Nettchen Stern's neighbor who had committed suicide, would sooner or later kill herself in her kitchen regardless of the persecution of the Jews. As if all the Jewish lawyers and doctors in Germany who had ended their own lives during the Nazi period (and there were many) did so because they were inherently depressed and not because they had been deprived of the essence of life—hope.[3]

In contrast to those who found all the answers in physiology and heredity, other voices were emerging in Germany. While Lucie and Hugo wandered around Düsseldorf, a professor named Walter von Baeyer at the Department of Psychiatry at the University of Heidelberg (three hours south of here) was beginning to develop with his colleagues a more holistic approach that recognized the importance of social and environmental factors. He objected to the attempt to explain everything as inherent and did not believe that psychiatry could only be based on precise measurement methods. Von Baeyer had a liberal outlook and introduced a new spirit to his relations with his subordinates. For example, it was customary in Heidelberg that when the head of the department entered the room, everyone stood up, but von Baeyer discontinued this practice. I learned this from Professor Heinz Häfner, who worked with von Baeyer and co-authored a book with him about the psychology of the persecuted. This book was based on, among other things, 240 interviews that Häfner conducted with concentration camp survivors and recognized the destructive impact of persecution, especially in cases of severe rootlessness and prolonged mental traumatization.[4]

So this is what happened: Coffee was poured. The frogs were squirting, the kids were looking, Hugo was sitting in the hotel room, Lucie was shopping, Panse and von Baeyer were arguing, and my mom was sitting at home worrying, not knowing that one day she would find herself in the middle of the argument between them.

On Saturday, Hugo and Lucie went to Cologne with their friends the Pincoffs to visit the famous cathedral. Two years earlier, in 1954, an Italian chemist had visited the headquarters of the Bayer company near Cologne and posed his questions in fluent German. Someone remarked that it was rare to meet Italians who spoke German. "My name is Levi," the chemist said, "I'm a Jew, and I learned your language in Auschwitz." There were a stuttering apology and a long silence. It was Primo Levi who, as we know, was not only a famous author, but also an industrial chemist and had visited Germany several times on business. Levi was in a fighting mood at the time, walking around with a short-sleeved shirt that revealed the number tattooed on his arm. He had been working for the Italian paint company Siva for six years, and a year before the incident at Bayer, he had been promoted to become the technical director of the company. Perhaps there's another lesson here about Hugo Mendel: As opposed to Primo Levi who returned to Germany as a victor—despite everything you did to me, I'm here—my grandfather Hugo felt defeated. Lucie and Hugo just wanted out. Lucie spent their last days in Düsseldorf packing their suitcases, and she couldn't wait for the moment they would be out of Germany. On Wednesday they sent an express letter to my mother so that she would have their address in Zurich. "Düsseldorf isn't what it used to be," Lucie wrote, "and I am not sad to leave." And Hugo wrote that they were glad to leave Düsseldorf behind, and he tried to hide the storm inside him. Only a few drops from that storm found their way to his letter when he asked my mother to write often, and he underlined his request with three lines and added two exclamation marks.

30 ZURICH

"WILL YOU TEACH ME HEBREW?"

And so, as in 1933, they were back in Switzerland. A neutral territory that gave them time to gather their thoughts. They stayed at the Hotel de Theatre, and Lucie reported the presence of a phone and a radio in every room and that a piece of chocolate is left by their bed in the evening. My sister had just started first grade, and Oma wrote to her how happy she was with Eva's first steps in school, and suddenly she asked, "Will you teach me Hebrew?" as if she wanted to turn a new leaf in Israel, and this time, not as a part stranger. Instead of the German expression *"meine Geliebten"* (my loved ones) that opened many of her postcards, she opens a postcard from Switzerland with a mixture of German and Hebrew: *"geliebten sche lanu."*[1]

"I was happy to leave Germany," she wrote. "It's impossible to start there again, unless you *have* to be there or you are willing to assimilate." And Hugo wrote that although there are Jews who think differently, there is no way to maintain normal relationships with the Germans. "But all this is theoretical," he added, "because, from the beginning, we didn't have any plans to stay in Germany."

And now it was Lucie's turn to hit the Germans with the final stroke: "...and besides, in Germany, I haven't seen any elegant people," she wrote. In Düsseldorf there were only *"Mariechen und Klärchen"* ("simple" women), she added, unlike in Zurich—an elegant city where people didn't all look alike.

* * *

In the evening, I ask the receptionist at the Hotel de Theatre about the hotel's history. I want to make sure that this is where my grandparents stayed. She's not sure about it but offers to refer me to the manager. And suddenly, I don't care anymore. I am tired. What difference does it make?

I go out to take a walk on *Bahnhofstraße*, passing by stores that have never meant much to me—Chanel, Cartier, Rolex. In the distance, I see a streetcar approaching. Its bottom is painted blue, and its top is off-white, and a vague memory comes to mind. I have been here before. I completely forgot that I visited Zurich with my mom and my sister when I was a teenager. I don't remember anything from the visit to the city except that I got off the streetcar at the wrong stop and that I walked to the next station, where I met my mother and my sister. It was in 1970. My mother wanted us to get a taste of Europe. I always remembered our visit to Italy and France and the Swiss Alps (where I saw snow for the first time in my life), but somehow the Zurich part had vanished. Now that I think about it, were we on a similar mission back then? Did my mom visit Zurich in an attempt to understand what I am trying to understand?

Only upon my return from this whole trip would I realize that our 1970 visit to Zurich wasn't part of an inquiry but more of a finale.

31 RAPPERSWIL

"THERE'S A HARD DAY AHEAD OF YOU."

After two days in Zurich, they moved to Rapperswil, a picturesque town along the lake. Zurich can be expensive, they noted. They found a beautiful hotel on the water (and marked their room with an arrow on the postcard), and because it was off season and they were almost the only visitors, they enjoyed the extra attention, as all the waiters were fighting over who was going to serve the Mendels. Back in 1933, after they'd left Hamm, Lucie and the kids stayed in Weggis, another charming small town about an hour from Rapperswil, while Hugo went to the south of Germany to purchase the equipment for his factory. Maybe Lucie and Hugo avoided Weggis now, not to be reminded how optimistic and hopeful they had been before moving to Palestine.

Now they felt comfortable enough to speak to strangers. "From the other table they told us that they were in Lugano today and sweated like crazy, but when they drove to the mountains, there was snow there," Lucie wrote—the first time she reported a conversation with someone who wasn't necessarily Jewish.

Coffee, cakes, a hike along the lake, great service, and behind it all, a sadness that is hard to disguise. "If the good Lord will let us go to Europe again in our lifetime, we certainly will not do it without you," Lucie promised. And she ended her letter touching my mother's pain as the third anniversary of my dad's death was approaching: "There's a hard day ahead of you, my beloved Mirjam. I wish we could be there, and we are there, of course, in our thoughts."

On October 15 (which was the day my father died three years earlier), Lucie and Hugo boarded a Swissair plane and flew back to Tel Aviv. There, on the short table in their apartment, they prepared the gifts they'd brought us, including a bath sponge in the shape of an elephant.

32 TEL AVIV
"WE DON'T GO TO ALLENBY."

On Purim 1957, my mom took only Eva to the city for the traditional picture taking. Maybe I was sick, but a more likely explanation is that the anxiety at 5 Reines Street had reached such a level that my mother decided to leave me with one of our neighbors. My sister was a ballerina that year. She held the edges of her tutu and looked at someone who stood beside the photographer. Someone later suggested that they all go see the Purim parade on Allenby Street, and Hugo said, "We don't go to Allenby."

Not much is known about what happened to Hugo after their return in October, but my uncle Raphi, who was abroad, remembered getting reports from Tel Aviv that things were not good. Just two weeks after they'd returned, the Sinai campaign started.[1] The windows were covered with thin black cardboard to prevent any lights that might be detected by Egyptian bombers from coming through. And before the lights were turned on at night, Lucie lowered the shutters all the way down so that no ray of light would escape. When the fear of the first few days made room for the pride in Israel's victory, Hugo did not join the celebration. He rarely left the apartment.

On the third of January 1957, Hugo cut out an article from the German newspaper that announced that small business owners such as doctors and lawyers who had been forced to leave Germany because they were Jewish may receive compensation for the reputation that their business had built. The newspaper used the English term "goodwill" to explain the concept, and Hugo wrote, almost etched, the word on the piece of newspaper twice: "Goodwill. Goodwill." A few days later, on January 9, the neurologist Dr. Ben Uriah Lowenstein saw him. Hugo complained of a tremble in his left hand, and Dr. Lowenstein diagnosed it as atherosclerosis with Parkinson-like symptoms. A couple of weeks before Purim, Hugo and Lucie went to another neurologist, Dr. Siegfried Steckelmacher on Bialik Street, who would remember a pre-aged patient with hypochondriac thoughts and a tremor in his left hand.

I learned about these medical examinations from the folder Mechtild had given me. Another document I found in the boxes I'd brought from my mom's house was Hugo's Israeli passport that perhaps best tells what had happened between his return to Israel and his death. At some point, the passport was violently ripped at the seam, maybe in rage by a torn man who no longer wanted to hear from anyone. If anyone calls, tell them I died, and not only those who call during nap time, but almost everyone. Maybe it will make them think about why they haven't called earlier. And slowly the circle tightens, and the "almost" becomes smaller and smaller to a point where he says: "If anyone calls, even Mirjam, tell her I died."

* * *

On March 19, 1957, two days after my sister's picture as a ballerina was taken, Hugo decided to end his life. (Actually, do people decide on such things in the morning and execute around lunchtime? I don't know.) When my mom told me about the suicide, 30 years later, she said she thought that when he said, "We don't go to

Allenby," it was because he'd already picked the building on Allenby Street where he would do it.

My sister, who was six, remembers that one day, as our mom was putting her earrings on in the bathroom, she said, while still looking in the mirror:

"Opa fell down the stairs, and he's in the hospital."

After a few days, Eva asked how Opa was doing, and my mother answered impatiently that he was still in the hospital. The next time that my sister asked, my mom answered quickly as if she had been rehearsing the line and was waiting for the occasion:

"He fell down the stairs, and he died." End of story. It would take my sister about 30 years to find out what had really happened, but for now, the explanation was sufficient. I was so young that I didn't even realize that an explanation was called for.

* * *

Early morning in Tel Aviv, and I decide to find the building where Hugo killed himself. I know that it's in a place on Allenby Street called Passage Tamar, the 1950s version of a shopping mall. The city is quiet, and a man hoses the sidewalk in front of his store. I find a building that looks like the passage. I enter the old building that has seen better days. The stores with archaic signs are still closed: a watchmaker, a hearing aid store, a travel agency. A door of an insurance office is open, and I peek in. A man in his 50s is sitting behind a cheap desk; its laminate is peeling.

"Is this Passage Tamar?" I ask him.

"This is Passage Tamar. Who are you looking for?" he asks.

For a moment, I consider telling him, but I just thank him, and as I turn, I detect the stairs—at the other corner of the building. I take the stairs to the third floor and look down at that point of contact. It isn't a sidewalk as in the joke I told my mother, but a floor of marble tiles that was probably shiny that day.

* * *

A thought hits me as I'm sitting at my desk in Menlo Park a few months after my return from Tel Aviv. I push the thought away, but it keeps returning. I know that Hugo ended his life on Allenby Street, and I know that my mom worked on Allenby Street at the time. *So what?* I think to myself; it's a long street. But I have to check the house numbers. I find online that Passage Tamar is located at III Allenby Street. I reach for the folder that Mechtild gave me with some paperwork from Dr. Lichtenstein and look at the address on his letterhead: 112 Allenby, two minutes from there. Did Hugo stop at my mom's office before he did it? Did he say anything? Did she reply? Did she hear people yelling that someone had fallen from the third floor? Did she hear the sirens? Did she go to the window to find out what was happening? Did she run there?

33 TEL AVIV
"FOR HIS TRAGIC DEATH."

"You handled the funeral arrangements," Ruth Grossman asks her husband, Benjamin, without a question mark. They've been together for so many years (more than 60 according to my calculation), and there's efficient tenderness between them that can make punctuation marks superfluous.

"Yes, and I went to identify him," he adds. If some picture flashes in front of his eyes from his visit to the morgue, it doesn't find its way to his face, which stays impassive. His hair is thinning, and his face is fleshy and red. Ruth's hair is black like a raven, and her face is pale. Ruth is the daughter of Harry Binheim and his wife, Käthe, (Lucie's sister), which means that she's my mom's first cousin. But she wasn't just her cousin—she was also one of her best friends. Both my mom and Ruth brought home "Polish" men (who received a warm welcome by their parents, despite the *Yekkes'* snobbishness). Both were good marriages, Ruth's very long, my mom's very short.

I'm sitting at the Grossmans' dining area in Givatayim, near Tel Aviv. It's hot outside, the shutters are closed, and it's cool inside. Before he retired, Benjamin was an engineer at the Israel Electric Corporation, and when I was a kid, the Grossmans' house looked to me like a mansion—with a living room that was considered spacious and something I never encountered at the time—stairs inside the house that led to the bedrooms on the second floor. Benjamin is drinking tea while listening to the radio in the kitchen, occasionally approaching us to answer one of Ruth's questions or to report the latest news. The phone keeps interrupting us, and now it rings again. Wrong number.

"What's with the phone today?" Ruth grumbles, and I can close my eyes and hear my mom. I recall again my mom's friend who told me that she misses my mom so much that she finds herself "chasing old *Yekke* ladies," and this is why I chase Ruth Grossman. I'm here today so that she can help me translate letters of condolences, some of them scribbled in impossible handwriting.

We're wondering why Benjamin had to handle the funeral arrangements and not Raphi, my mom's brother.

"I'll ask him tomorrow," I say, "but I think he was abroad."

"He was abroad," Ruth remembers, or maybe just echoes my words.

The following day Raphi will confirm that indeed he was in New York, and this is why the funeral arrangements fell to Benjamin. Everything else fell on my mom's shoulders: from the security deposit for the sheet that covered Hugo's body to the ad in the *Yekke* newspaper. And another thing landed on her shoulders, like a clumsy, heavy bird: guilt. And with the instinct of someone who feels such a bird tangling in her clothes, my mom, and Oma too, told everyone (and not only Eva) that Hugo had fallen down the stairs. Because if he fell, then he fell—a misfortune. But if he jumped, his jump can be interpreted not only as an act of desperation but also as an admission that his life had been in vain. And if his life had failed, maybe they were partners to this failure, and to toss away the shame in such partnership, the official version emerged: Hugo fell down the stairs. He got dizzy and fell. That's it. And to make sure no one got the wrong idea from sensational newspapers, my mom talked to a couple of her friends who were well-connected in the police and the media, and after some calls and intercessions, she felt that she'd done everything in her power to save, if only slightly, her dad's honor.

Ruth reads me a letter of condolence from Trude and Hugo Aschenberg, relatives from New York who had heard the bad news from Ernst and Hilde Katzenstein who happened to be in the United States. Trude Aschenberg recalled the engagement party of Hugo and Lucie in Northeim: "How happy we were back then, and how many!" she wrote. Ernst Katzenstein wrote from New York that he did not imagine that their meeting in Frankfurt would be the last time he'd seen Hugo. (Ruth recalls that when she was a little girl in Hamelin, Ernst Katzenstein, who was their neighbor, would complain to her parents: "It's OK that Ruth sings during nap time, but why under my window?"). Mary and Franz Fürstenberg recalled in their letter the beautiful days they'd had together in Wiesbaden and Frankfurt, and Mary added that things were not that great with her husband either. Since the beginning of the winter, Franz had had high blood pressure and a bladder infection. It is good that Hugo had a chance to see Europe, which he had loved so much, and it's good that it ended this way at once, with no pain.[1] Benjamin Grossman comes from the kitchen and continues to report the news: There was a terrorist attack in the city of Afula in the north of Israel.

* * *

Hugo died on a Tuesday, and the following day at 3:15 in the afternoon, the funeral left the Hadassah Hospital for the cemetery. For the second time in four years, my mom walked behind a dead man she loved. I assume that the following day she was with her mom at the apartment on Reines Street, and I don't know whether someone brought them the papers or whether she went to the newsstand to get them. I'm sure though that she was shocked when she read the newspaper reports about Hugo Mendel, a 66-year-old man who had jumped from the third floor to the bottom of the stairwell in a building in Tel Aviv. A police car took him to the municipal hospital where he died an hour later. Only *Yediot Aharonot,* one of Israel's largest newspapers, cooperated with my mom: "At first, the police believed that this was a suicide, but further investigation proved that the deceased was looking for an office in the building, and since he suffers from dizziness, he stumbled and fell down the stairs."[2] Another bombshell fell on Reines 5 when a condolence ad from some distant relatives used the term "tragic death," the common code for suicide. So that was it. This was how Hugo Mendel would be remembered, and my mom was left with the burden of yet another failure.

34 TEL AVIV
"IT WAS NO PICNIC."

Purim 1958, and we again stood on the small stage at Photo Gilai—a young sailor who obediently looked at the camera and a Chinese girl with a tiny smile. I remember a world of women. The men— my father and Hugo—would be present for a few more years through their safety razors that for some reason, were left in the bathrooms, but then those disappeared as well. Raphi was usually traveling, and we would meet the other men of the family on holidays, and they would ask me about school. I managed pretty well without men. My mom's guru in raising us was Dr. Benjamin Spock, who argued in his book that a boy who grows up without a father needs to play as much as possible with other boys. And I did. I convinced my next-door neighbor Udi, who was a year younger than I, that if we were to get on a bench and flap our hands fast enough, we might take off like birds. We knew that it was a long shot, and the more we tried, the more we knew it. Next, we opened a hotel in his guava tree and served the preserving liquid from canned pickles as soup. I learned from an older boy how to pee standing up, another teenage boy taught me how to ride my bike, and I spent most of my afternoons playing cowboys and Indians, throwing cypress fruit at other boys and starting ambitious projects in our backyard: digging a pool, starting a circus, sending a rocket to the moon. I was a popular kid, and although I was terrible at sports, the kids elected me again and again to be a team leader. This ended abruptly after I accidentally threw a heavy ball vertically instead of horizontally and my teammates had had to run for their lives.

Years later, when we had our own kids, I wrote to my mom how amazed I was that she had raised us on her own. She wrote back, "It was no picnic," and she remembered always being tired and short on cash, but she added that I shouldn't forget that she had plenty of help from Oma, Opa, and Ora. ("Funny how you change only one letter," my mom commented.) Ora was our beloved cleaning lady who would come twice a week from a faraway neighborhood and would tell Eva and me stories about her life in faraway Yemen. She certainly deserves to be on that list. I'm bewildered by Opa's inclusion in this support group, as he vanished from our lives when I was four, but my sister remembers him bringing us *Shabbos bonbons* (Shabbat candy) on Saturdays and showering us with love. There were also several neighbors who assisted, but there is no doubt that Oma did more than anyone else to help my mom raise us.

I could spend hours in Oma's small apartment, playing with old wires, burnt fuses, and a box of magic tricks. When I would get bored with this, I would pull down the hinged yellow door where I would find Hugo's folding camera, a writing block, colors, a piano tuning fork, and dozens of green envelopes printed with the address of Hugo's law firm. And once I would get bored with this, we would play a game of checkers, or she would read to me about the adventures of Max and Moritz or about the horrifying things that happen to kids who misbehave in *Struwwelpeter*. Oma also would often come to our house in the suburbs on the weekend. She would arrive at our doorstep with a bag of pistachio nuts and her cheerful spirit. I loved taking walks with her in the fields that surrounded our neighborhood almost as much as I loved the walks with her in the city. After lunch, when my mom would take her nap, Oma would put a folding chair on the lawn and uproot some weeds. When she would be done with one area of the lawn, she would move the chair to another area and keep going. Upon special request, she would cut a long blade of grass and play the trumpet or tell me about the latest in the big city.

One time, she told me that when she'd boarded the bus to come to us—a black dog followed her and sat next to her on the floor. The bus driver explained to her that dogs were not allowed and asked her to take the dog off the bus. Oma told him that this was not her dog. The bus driver didn't believe her and insisted that she take the dog immediately off the bus. Oma raised her voice and gave him a piece of her mind. The driver reverted to the default ultimatum of bus drivers and announced that the bus was not going anywhere as long as the dog remained on board. Other passengers started to get upset at Oma. Just when the situation seemed to reach a dead end, the dog ran out of the bus, possibly after a cat. A few weeks later, when Oma came to visit us, I asked her if anything unusual had happened on her way. She said that she couldn't believe it, but that the same black dog followed her again this time, and she repeated a very similar story with another bus driver. This driver too assumed it was Oma's dog. Again, Oma denied ownership; the driver did not believe her, and so on. A few weeks followed, and Oma came to visit us again. Even before she'd pulled the pistachio nuts out of her tote bag, I asked her whether anything had happened, and Oma said that as amazing as it may sound, the whole thing repeated itself. I was fascinated as she described every detail, but a seed of doubt sprouted inside me. When she finished, I had to ask: "Oma, is it true?"

"No," she said, and there was no apology in her voice.

I asked her some more questions, and with each answer, the depth of the deceit became clearer. I was willing to accept that she had repeated the story for the third time just to make me happy. Maybe even that it hadn't happened for the second time, but when I realized that it never had happened at all, I felt cheated. No dog had ever followed her on a bus. No driver got upset. Nothing.

"It's just a story," Oma said.

"But it isn't true!"

I tell the black dog story because this whole issue of stories and concealments is on my mind. We didn't know about Opa's suicide as kids. We also didn't know about Nettchen's death, and Oma pretended to be this happy-go-lucky girl who used a blade of grass as a trumpet. But maybe it was better that way; after all, we were kids, and our role was to inject happiness into their lives. Besides, after a lot of thinking, I have concluded that if you peeled away the cheerful version of Oma, you would find a pretty happy person. So I don't think that Oma, as we knew her, was just a story.

Still, it annoys me how little I knew. After all, what happened to Nettchen and what happened to Hugo clearly were always on her shoulders, pecking at her occasionally. What if I did this? What if I said something else? Maybe Nettchen would not have gone back to Germany? Maybe Hugo would not have gone to Allenby? I was clueless about her pain. And also about her earthly troubles: for example, the fact that Oma brought us pistachio nuts (which I already knew were more expensive than peanuts or sunflower seeds) made her a millionaire in my mind. But the truth was far different. The monthly allowance Hugo got from the Germans for the loss of his profession was cut by 40 percent after his death, and Lucie found it hard to support herself. And the hardship was followed by small insults. Before Hugo died, a lawyer by the name of Adlerstein had started helping him with two other claims from the Germans. One was for the deterioration in his health, and the other one was for the goodwill in his business. These claims were still active after his death, and one day, Lucie went to the lawyer's office to get an update.

Adlerstein was away, and his assistant told Lucie that they didn't know where things stood regarding her claims. Yet just before leaving, Lucie noticed a handwritten note on her file indicating that they believed her case was hopeless. Flustered and hurt, she stormed out of the place. In cases like this, it was my mom who would be on the receiving end of Oma's pain, and I can imagine her frustration as she was typing a letter of protest on behalf of her mother to Dr. Adlerstein demanding an explanation: Why was it a hopeless case? I assume that my mom considered moving the case to her boss, Dr. Lichtenstein, but he specialized in the Danzig community, and maybe she didn't dare ask him to take the case or thought that it was inappropriate. Here she was failing again. Not only did everyone know that her father had died a "tragic death," but she, who was helping the Jews of Danzig every day, could not help her own mom.

In the end, everything fell on my mom's shoulders: her mother, my sister and I, Tante Liese, the clients at her office, her father's death and maybe Nettchen's death too. And it showed. My mother was easily irritated, and sometimes the temper that we all inherited from Onkel Max would come out as she would scream at us in German: *"Herr Jesus noch mal!"* (Jesus Christ!)[1] At times, she would be defeated: She would close the shutters, herself, and the door to her room, and lie on her bed in the dark, and we would know that she had a migraine and that we shouldn't even whisper. After a few hours, she would come out of her bedroom, say "It's better" when we asked how she was doing, and make us dinner. She was smoking a pack a day and never stopped picking on the skin around her fingernails. One time her left finger got so infected that she told us she had asked Dr. Lichtenstein to avoid words with the letters R, T, and B in his correspondence.

Her dry humor helped her and left little room for us to experience pain together. If I got hurt, she would say, "It will be gone by your wedding" (she was right). If I argued with her, she would ask, "Am *I* the mother, or are *you* the son?" We didn't have long, meaningful conversations, but her one-liners were comforting, like a diner jukebox that plays the song of the button you pushed. If I said that the food was hot, she would say that she didn't know how to cook cold. If I started a sentence with "I think..." she would cut me off: "Leave the thinking to the horses. They have large heads." When I was too silly, she would start talking to herself about Mrs.

Steinmann, an acquaintance who had been committed to a mental hospital: "Yeah... this is how it started for Mrs. Steinmann too." When I got bronchitis and said that it hurt when I breathed, she would shoot back with "so don't breathe." When she would put her head on the pillow at night, I would hear her saying, "This is the moment I've been waiting for" (which my wife and I still say when our heads touch our pillows after an exceptionally hectic day).

* * *

In the summer, my mother would pack a couple of books in English and her bathing suit, and she would take us for a week's vacation in the Ben Yehuda Hotel in Haifa where she could stay at a discount as an officer's widow. She would sit for hours by the pool, reading, while my sister and I would be in the water. One afternoon in Haifa, my mother took me to see the new technological miracle of Israel: the Carmelit. It was the first subway in Israel that connected the harbor area with Mount Carmel. After an uneventful ride on the subway, we approached another innovation we had never encountered before—an escalator. I didn't fully understand what was unfolding there in front of my eyes, how these steps could suddenly appear from nowhere and, after a few moments of glory, disappear into the floor. Apparently, neither did my mother, but she marched forward confidently to demonstrate how it was done and stepped right on the crack between two steps. Next thing I saw was my stunned mother lying flat on the moving escalator. I was sure she was going to disappear at the top in the slot where the steps vanish. That's it. I was going to be an orphan and not a very dignified one. My father, an officer in the army, died of a heart attack, not in battle. And my mother? Eaten by an escalator. My mother's mind was occupied, as she would confide in me later, with a more realistic concern. She was sure that her dress would get caught in some metal part or a screw, and she was already imagining herself running in her underwear to one of the nearby stores to buy something to cover herself. At the last minute, a young man who was a few steps ahead of her on the stairs ran down the escalator, and as a true *Kavalier,* helped my mother get up. We couldn't thank him enough, and my mother would not step again on an escalator for more than 20 years.

The whole experience nearly overnight turned into one of the most popular family stories—how mom had fallen up the moving stairs. Much more popular than the story that was never mentioned again about Opa who had fallen down the stairs. The words Hugo or Opa or *Vati* (dad) were hardly ever mentioned in the little apartment on Reines Street or in our house. Yet underneath it all was a current of shame and insult that this is how the life of Dr. Hugo Mendel had ended.

35 JERUSALEM
"LUCIE WENT WITH THE FLOW."

As I drive around Raphi's neighborhood near Jerusalem looking for his apartment, people examine my car with suspicion. A suicide bomber had blown himself up yesterday in Afula, a city in the north. "Relax," I tell the eyes that examine me. "I'm here about a different suicide." On the way here, I stopped at a shopping mall to buy deodorant, and a guard checked my bag at the entrance. He was a big guy with a heavy Russian accent.

"Any weapons?" he asked, a question he utters a thousand times a day.

"No," I said, and he groped the bottom of my backpack. Back in Russia, he may have been an engineer or a chemist.

* * *

Raphi opens the door, trying to control an over-friendly curly dog that almost reaches my face to lick me. We've been talking on the phone, but I haven't seen Raphi for several years, and I'm a bit shocked to see him. He's approaching 80, suffers from Parkinson's, and is a bit bent. It takes a few moments before I see through his current image, the handsome uncle with the pipe who knew how to wiggle his ears, (which have grown significantly). He's wearing the same thick-framed glasses he's always worn, combing his thinning hair to the side. He still looks dignified. When he was seen around Israeli embassies or delegations, more than once people mistook him for Abba Eban, Israel's minister of Foreign Affairs.

We sit at the dining table in the small apartment. Raphi remembers an air of haughtiness in the Mendel household in Hamm. If he brought home a friend who wasn't up to the family's standard, someone would say, "A Mendel writes on better paper." They made fun of *Kafers*, provincial people who were embodied in the character of a cleaning lady who always said, "What the farmer does not know, he does not eat." They looked down at the nouveau riche like the butcher's wife who used to complain, "I spent the whole day polishing the sterling silverware." They looked down at Yiddish, which they saw as butchered German. The word *Ostjuden* in itself was taboo, but they did feel that they were better than the Jews from the East who didn't know how to properly pronounce words with umlauts like *Stück* (piece) or *Vögel* (birds).

And with every group they looked down at, they lifted themselves away. They were not *Kafers*, they were not *Ostjuden*, and they were not nouveau riche. They were members of an exclusive club that walked around with two glowing umlaut dots over their heads, speaking appropriate German, commanding perfect table manners, and experimenting with new foods in faraway places such as Paris. They were on top of the world. Maybe it was that height that made their fall so deadly.

Raphi remembers his father, Hugo, walking in a hot summer day in Tel Aviv, wearing a suit and a tie, occasionally stopping to take off his straw hat and move his thumb along the inner band to wipe the sweat that had accumulated there. "Hugo lived the way life was supposed to be," Raphi says, and I remember the poem that Gertrud Katz had read to me in New York about the need to sometimes bend.

Perhaps this was the thing. Hugo grew up with one schema of how things were supposed to be, and he expected to walk through it straight and upright. When he faced a new world order, he never managed to bend. Oma was different. "Lucie went with the flow of life," Raphi says. "She didn't try to change things but accepted the situations she faced and tried to make the best out of them." There's often some bending in adjusting.

This fits with the Oma I knew. And I don't remember her as a snob. Yes, she had her prejudices, but she liked people and was curious about them. She had great respect for my father's parents, even though they were *Ostjuden* from Poland. She wasn't shy about peppering her talk with occasional Yiddish. Maybe this is why Oma felt much more Israeli than Hugo did. She never liked the shouting on the street or people cutting in line, but she accepted it as part of the territory.

I think about the Russian guy who'd checked my bag at the mall this morning. How is he doing bending? I guess it has to do with how much being an engineer was part of who he was in Russia. Was he Boris the engineer? Or Boris, the father who's also an engineer? Or Boris, who loves feeding blue jays, who's also a father and an engineer? And I guess it also has to do with how important it is to him what other people think. Most people feel that a guard at a shopping mall is not as important as the engineer who had planned the construction of that mall. Most people feel that selling fences is less honorable than appearing in court to defend the burglars who'd cut those fences. It has to do with pride. If there's some bending in adjusting, the proudest won't adjust.

Raphi's Parkinson's is not a new thing; he's had it for years, but it seems to me that the tremor has become worse. He opened the door by himself, but most of the time he's sitting, his head tilted sideways, and a friendly woman from the Philippines named Violetta helps around the house. He speaks clearly, playing with the pipe in his hand. I was the proudest kid when he once let me borrow one of his pipes for a Purim costume. With Hugo's camera over my shoulder, Raphi's pipe in my mouth, and a suitcase in my hand, Oma turned me into a tourist. (Or maybe it was my mom who had designed my costume that year?) Raphi tells me how he found out about his Parkinson's years ago. He was abroad and went to a physician for some routine checkup. Before he left, the doctor asked him how he was handling his Parkinson's. Raphi had no idea what he was talking about, but the physician said that he could tell by the way Raphi was walking that he had the disease. This was 15 years ago, and Raphi learned to accept his condition and live with it. Hugo was never diagnosed as having Parkinson's, but he'd had a tremor in the last year of his life, and maybe he decided to die so that he would not be a burden as his condition progressed. Maybe he didn't understand the weighty burden his suicide would be.

Raphi doesn't talk much about his days in the Mossad, but at the archive in Hamm, I found that he'd registered as a resident in the early 1950s. I suppose that being a German citizen helped when he headed one of the Mossad's units that hunted down Nazi war criminals. From an article in an Israeli newspaper, I learn that he was in charge of the contact with Fritz Bauer, the Jewish German district attorney of the state of Hessen who gave Israel information regarding the whereabouts of Adolf Eichmann, the Nazi who managed the logistics of mass deportation of Jews to ghettos and extermination camps. In May 1960, Raphi's colleagues captured Eichmann in Argentina and brought him to Israel, and his trial began in Jerusalem in April 1961.[1]

Like everyone else in Israel, my mother bought a transistor radio and would listen to the live broadcasts of Eichmann's trial. It was a strange and gloomy spring. My mother would leave for work in the morning with the transistor in her hand. At night, I remember her standing by the sink, washing the dishes after dinner, listening to the daily summary of the trial. Raphi was in Israel, rushing from task to task, and he tells me how once before the trial had begun, he arrived at the prosecutor Gideon Hausner's office to find the man practicing his opening remarks. Hausner invited Raphi to stay and listen to his famous Six Million Accusers speech.

I didn't hear the trial itself. Some kids talked about it, and the brave ones drew a swastika in the sand and erased it instantly or drew one on a piece of paper and then connected the lines to transform it into a square window with metal bars.

How Lucie reacted to the trial, I do not remember. But I can imagine that, as with so many others, it scratched the thin scab off her wound. The deportations of German Jews to Riga had been carried out as a personal initiative of Eichmann, and he visited there several times. I don't know if she or my mom heard the testimony of Eliezer Karstadt from Riga who told the court about the executions. "There was a German there with a machine gun. They would dig trenches, put down their personal belongings, and whoever was lucky, would get a bullet and die; those who weren't lucky would be thrown into the trenches and suffocate alive."

The dozens of testimonies communicated not only the extent of the horror but also its complexity and the fact that there was more than one way to be a victim of the Holocaust. True, the typical victims were those who were gassed in the camps, or they were people like Nettchen, who were shot or who starved to death or got sick in the camps and ghettos. But what about those, like Nettchen's neighbor, Mrs. Waller, who couldn't deal with the emotional stress and chose to end their own lives? Benno Cohen, one of the leaders of the German Jewish community, testified one day at Eichmann's trial about the extent of the suicide phenomenon among the German Jews: "We received the gloomy reports from all the cities that a certain lawyer, a certain physician, this industrialist, or that big trader had committed suicide; they couldn't stand the pain they'd been caused as a result of losing their status and their honor. They didn't understand what happened and chose this way," Cohen said.[2]

My mom was washing the dishes and listening. These people were victims of the Nazis too. Her father reacted exactly as they had.

36 NICOSIA
"AUF WIEDERSEHEN."

On August 14, the Eichmann trial ended, and two days later, as if they were gasping for some fresh air, Oma, my mom, and Tante Liese took us to Cyprus. Oma did not forget her dream of showing us the beauty of Europe, but such a trip was beyond her means, and perhaps she was afraid of repeating her experience from 1956. Cyprus was a hot destination for Israelis in 1961, and the three women took advantage of some great deal. We flew to Nicosia, which was so crowded with Israelis that local merchants displayed signs in Hebrew. My family's longing for Europe drove them away from Israelis. We stayed at some remote hotel surrounded by trees, away from the crowds, and on the second day, Oma got food poisoning. My mom called a doctor through the hotel, and when he arrived, the guy was happy to chat with the three ladies in German, a language that he had studied in college. He didn't seem too concerned by Oma's condition, prescribed some medication, and at the door he said, *"Auf Wiedersehen,"* which means good-bye and literally means, "until we see each other again." My mom wasn't happy about that, and after he'd left, she kept muttering about his choice of words.

"We don't want to see him again," she said.

His *Auf Wiedersehen* was bugging her during the next few days. With her luck, something terrible was bound to happen. Still, she managed to enjoy the week, and they tried to capture every drop of Europe that Cyprus could offer. Their greatest pleasure was to see my sister and me take our first steps into Western civilization—our first bottle of Coca Cola, the first TV show we watched, the first time we said, "Thank you" in English. We felt like real jet setters. We bought a steam iron, we took a trip on a tourist bus, and we visited a monastery—all new experiences. When our bus got stuck on a narrow road with another bus facing it, and our driver had to back up a few hundred meters, my mom was sure that this was it, we were going to roll into the abyss and, if we were lucky and didn't die instantly, meet Dr. *Auf Wiedersehen*. But no, we survived the drive and, as always, the calamity came from an unexpected angle —a day before our flight back to Tel Aviv, the door of the taxi got slammed on Tante Liese's hand. The hotel called the German-speaking doctor; he suspected a broken bone and took Liese and my mom to the hospital. When Liese got back with a cast on her hand, my mother said, "I told him, 'no *Auf Wiedersehen* this time. *Guten Tag* (good day) is good enough.'"

That night, our last night in Cyprus, my mom slept in the same room with Tante Liese, and Oma slept in our room. We were talking with Oma about our return to Israel, and she told us about the royal reception we should expect at the airport. She stood up on her bed in her nightgown and walked up and down a red carpet, transforming in front of our eyes into a princess and then into a radio reporter who was interviewing Lucie Mendel upon her return, and—to our amazement—into the prime minister of Israel, David Ben Gurion himself who came to greet Oma personally. The encounter between Oma and Ben Gurion was especially funny to us because up to that moment, we had not even realized that Oma knew who Ben Gurion was. She was the entertainer who would blow the trumpet on blades of grass and bring pistachio nuts on the weekends, and he was the one running the country. And suddenly this? We were howling on the floor when a loud (yet restrained) knock was heard on the door. When Oma opened, it was the responsible grown-up—Mirjam Rosen—and the three of us were scolded. Tante Liese is in pain in the next room, and we are making such a commotion?

When my mom left the room, Oma got back on the red carpet, but she and Mr. Ben Gurion were now whispering their mutual greetings.

37 TEL AVIV

"MY FATHER NEVER BELONGED TO PALESTINE."

Maybe it was the Eichmann trial; perhaps it was the trip to Cyprus that energized my mom. At some point during these months, she decided that she must do something to ensure a decent income for her mother and, perhaps more importantly, that she must reclaim the lost honor of her father, even at the cost of public admission of his suicide. She talked to Oma and then with her boss. Even though Oma wasn't from Danzig as the rest of his clients were, Dr. Lichtenstein agreed to take the case. Not a claim for goodwill, not his health, but a claim for the loss of Dr. Hugo Mendel's life. As if the Nazis had killed him in the camps.

At the beginning of 1962, Dr. Lichtenstein and my mom got to work. My mom collected all the documents: Hugo's credentials, the letter that prohibited him from appearing in court, the letters Hugo and Lucie sent us from Germany. She removed the gray plastic cover from her Underwood typewriter and began writing. We, of course, had no idea what she was working on. A burning cigarette in the ashtray next to her, she would stop typing from time to time, draw from the cigarette, think, and then start typing again. Tak Tak Tak. Cough. Ratchety sound. Ring.

Together with Lucie, she wrote a statement on Lucie's behalf that described the whole story, how Hugo had built his law office from scratch in Hamm and about what happened when the Nazis took over. "The loss of the law practice that he had built with lots of love was a big shock for my husband, who wasn't one of those who easily overcome the blows of life," Lucie wrote. "Before we left, he was arrested twice by the Gestapo who were looking for lists of Jewish activists, and these arrests depressed him very much." Lucie described the immigration to Palestine, the mesh wire factory and its end, and how Hugo became a salesman in the firm that he had started. She also talked about her work at Café Palatin and noted how much this depressed Hugo, "...as it reflected our social decline in comparison to our status in Hamm."

Hugo was a salesman for 16 years. Only in April 1956, when he started to get a monthly allowance for the loss of his profession, did his economic situation improve, "but the years between 1933 and 1956 managed to destroy him physically and emotionally," they wrote. Then Lucie wrote about their trip to Germany and summed it up this way: "The visit to Germany did not improve my husband's situation, as I was hoping. On the contrary, it made it worse. His feeling that in fact he belonged in Germany, but that he could not go back, shocked him and worsened the depression that he had had for years."[1]

Finding a German lawyer who would represent my grandmother in Germany proved to be a challenge. Dr. Lichtenstein had good connections in Danzig but none in Westphalia. They wrote to Friedrich Kieserling in Hamm, but he pointed to a conflict of interest. They contacted another lawyer in Hamm and received a long letter explaining why the firm declined to take the case. The deadline for cases on death has expired, and it would be extremely hard to prove a link between the persecution in 1933 and the suicide in 1957. The chances of success were so slim that the firm didn't want to waste Mrs. Mendel's money. Besides, in earlier correspondence with the authorities, Lucie had stated that Hugo's death was an accident, so now they'd need to prove that it was a suicide. That lawyer expressed his willingness to help if they got stuck without representation, but his overall message was clear: The chances are close to zero.[2]

* * *

My mom was very proper. For example, I never heard her say the word shit. In English, that is. But she spoke four languages, and English was just one of them (and reserved for British pearls of wisdom such as "Charity begins at home," which I heard often). When she would get furious (tripping over a toy, for example), she would use the German "*Verdammte Scheiße!*" (Damned shit). For things that made her furious and disappointed, she would go with "*Scheiße!*" If her anger were more cerebral, she would switch to French: "*Merde!*" (which I think she'd picked up from Raphi). She used the Hebrew word *Chara* when expressing her opinion about the general political situation in Israel. I think that when she got the folder back from the lawyer in Hamm, it was a case of "*Scheiße!*"

* * *

The symphony of clicks, rings, and coughs intensified at our home as my mother wrote draft after draft of her own affidavit. "My father never belonged to Palestine, not economically, not culturally, and not emotionally," she wrote, and invoked the image of an old respected lawyer walking from one hardware store to the other, peddling his wares. "The loss of status associated with this was unbearable," she wrote. She detailed her parents' trip to Germany and described her father's returning to his homeland after 23 years as a stranger, rootless, homeless. She talked about the deterioration that she believed was caused by the trip and about the last months of his life when he was at home, depressed and anxious.[3] Lichtenstein wrote a letter of his own, wherein he supported my mom's argument. Yes, the monthly allowance you started paying him for the loss of his profession elevated his situation some, but this money did not give him a sense that he had regained control of his life. He knew that he wouldn't be able to go back to his position in Germany, and this truth became painfully clear when he visited Germany in 1956.

In May 1962, they sent the affidavits and all the material to Germany, and after some time, they received a case number from the LRB (the *Landesrentenbehörde*, the State Pension Office of North Rhine-Westphalia). This confirmation letter was followed by a long silence.[4]

38 ZURICH
"LET'S WAIT FOR YOUR DAUGHTER TO RETURN."

Almost a year after they had submitted their claim, still nothing had happened, and my mom went to Europe for the first time as an adult. This had nothing to do with the claim or with Germany. The idea for the trip arose when our neighbors Uzi and Sarah Yellin went to Italy, France, and Switzerland and invited my mother to come along. With her tight budget, two kids at home, a job, and a million other things to worry about, she said no, but someone made sure that it happened. On April 2, 1963, we went to Haifa to bring her to the ship "Moledet." My mom looked happy. With her sunglasses, thick dark hair, and a fashionable handbag, she looked like Jackie Kennedy (just no Onassis). We were allowed to board the ship to see the cabin she would share with Sarah (Uzi flew to Europe to combine it with a business trip). Once we had said good-bye, Oma and Raphi took us to eat hummus, and we also took the Carmelit. Oma's inquisitive mind didn't allow her to visit Haifa without checking out the *Rolltreppe* (rolling steps) that she had heard so much about. Unlike her daughter, she placed her foot at the right spot and ascended to the top like a princess. From there we went to Panorama Café, with its perfect view of the port, but the ship we were hoping to see had already sailed away.

As if the Germans were waiting for my mom to leave the country before replying to Lucie's claim, the response arrived at Dr. Lichtenstein's office a day after she had left. The LRB rejected the claim, as it didn't see a causal connection between the persecution and Hugo's suicide. It seemed that the Hamm lawyer who had declined to take the case was right after all. Dr. Lichtenstein sent Lucie a short letter informing her of the decision. "Let's wait until your daughter is back before we decide how to respond," he wrote.[1]

I can only guess how Lucie felt when she got his letter, but as kids, we didn't sense anything. Oma had moved to our house while my mom was abroad, and she had a detailed entertainment program that proceeded as planned. We went to see the German movie *The White Horse Inn,* and Oma enjoyed the songs so much that she started humming along with the cast, and my sister and I had to shush her. We ate lunch at a fancy hotel where we almost saw the Greek film star Aliki who, according to rumor, was staying there. This was Oma's greatness. True, she put a lot of her pain on my mother's shoulders, but she was less like an elephant who never forgets and more like a sponge that squeezes out the dirty water and soaks in the fresh pleasure of the moment.

Oma also enjoyed hearing every little detail about my mom's trip, and our red-faced sweating mailman quickly learned to pre-announce in German *"Post von Mirjam"* (letter from Mirjam) whenever he carried a letter from her because he knew how happy it made Mrs. Mendel. Once I read the correspondence between my mom and Oma during that trip, I understood that Oma was not only the one who pushed her daughter to take a break and go to Europe and volunteered to take care of us but also the one who'd financed it from her savings. Although so much was on my mom's shoulders, Oma was still her mom, and more than anything else, she wanted to see her daughter happy. My mother was grateful of course and did not stop thanking Oma in her letters. At some point, when the thank-you's got on Oma's nerves, she wrote, "If you write one more time that you could not have gone on this trip without me, you'll have me to answer to. My greatest pleasure is to be with them. When you are a grandma, you'll understand."

Among the postcards my mom sent from the trip, I found one from Zurich too, her parents' city of refuge and the only overlapping point of their trip and hers. And especially here, at the final destination of her parents' trip, I know how much she was thinking about them. What is taking the Germans so long? She has to secure her mother's future, and she has to help her father regain his dignity. When are the Germans going to respond?

39 TEL AVIV

"LUCIE MENDEL VS. THE STATE OF NORTH RHINE-WESTPHALIA."

When my mom returned from Europe, the answer was waiting on her desk, and she sat down right away to respond to the LRB, and in mid-May, Dr. Lichtenstein's office sent a well-argued appeal of the decision. This time the Germans were quick, and about a week later, they sent a letter that repeated, almost word for word, their previous decision: No. The suicide was not part of a chain of events that began in 1933.[1]

I imagine my mom getting up in the morning, getting us ready for school and walking to the bus station, while all that time, the big clumsy bird on her shoulder is screaming into her ear: Injustice! Injustice! There was an injustice done here that nobody was held responsible for, and she remembers the conversations she had with her dad that justice must be done. The bus arrives, and she finds a seat and looks out the window. Here's a young girl holding her dad's hand. To throw in the towel now would be to bury everything he had believed in. The bus arrives at the last stop, and she rushes on foot to the office on Allenby Street and talks to her lanky mentor. In the evening, she talks to Oma, and they agree to continue.

Continuing meant taking the state of North Rhine-Westphalia to court. Dr. Lichtenstein went to talk with another lawyer in Tel Aviv who recommended they get in touch with the lawyer Dr. Gert Dahlfeld from Duisburg. In August 1963, my mom wrote a long letter outlining the history of the case, and she and Dr. Lichtenstein sent it to Dr. Dahlfeld and asked him whether he would be willing to represent Lucie in this case. Dahlfeld agreed, and a few weeks later, a new case was opened in the Düsseldorf court known as *Lucie Mendel vs. the State of North Rhine-Westphalia*.[2]

Dahlfeld's report after the first court session was cautiously optimistic because he knew one of the judges as a fair person, and shortly after that meeting, the judges assigned a respected psychiatrist as an expert to state his opinion on the main question: Is there a reasonable link between the events of 1933 and Dr. Hugo Mendel's suicide in 1957?[3]

The expert was a famous professor from Düsseldorf named Dr. Panse.

40 MENLO PARK

"IS IT HIM?"

I'm sitting at my desk in Menlo Park trying to understand: Is it him? Is it the same Dr. Friedrich Panse who sent mentally ill patients to their deaths during Nazi time? It certainly looks that way, but it's hard for me to believe. His first name doesn't appear in the document from the court case I'm holding in my hand. Only the letters "Fr" appear before his name. Is it Friedrich? Or maybe it's Fred or Frank or some German honorific. Or maybe it's a different Friedrich Panse. Maybe a cousin who was also a psychiatrist. My German is not good enough to be sure I'm not combining some unrelated facts here.

I'm also holding a detailed article in English that was recently written by Dr. Ralf Forsbach, a professor at the Institute of Ethics, History, and Theory of Medicine at the University of Münster about Dr. Friedrich Panse (the one who sent patients to their deaths). I email Dr. Forsbach, attach a photo of the document from the file, and explain that I'm trying to find out whether the man who served as an expert witness in the trial regarding my grandfather Hugo Mendel is the same man who sent patients to their deaths.

A day passes and another day, and there is no response. According to Dr. Forsbach's article, in the second half of 1940, Panse served as a consultant on what is known as "Action T4," which was intended to improve the Aryan race by eliminating those who suffered from congenital malformations, chronic illnesses, or mental difficulties. As part of this, he assessed files from psychiatric institutions in Silesia and Austria and recommended the death of 15 patients. I also read that Panse was appointed to the Higher Genetic Health Court in Berlin, which had the final jurisdiction over appeals against sterilization orders, and that he'd taught classes on "racial hygiene" from 1937 until the end of the Nazi regime in 1945. Is this the man a German court chose as an expert witness for a case a Jewish widow had brought?

The more I read, the more I understand that selecting Dr. Panse as an expert witness (if it is the same Dr. Panse) has sealed the destiny of this case. From the article written by Dr. Forsbach, I learn that Panse believed that many soldiers he saw after WWI didn't really suffer from trauma but were pretending in order to receive state benefits. He also believed that German soldiers who were traumatized during the first World War were not entitled to any benefits because their suffering was typically the result of their "constitutional inferiority." A book I find at the library describes Panse as a prominent representative of the professional tradition that categorically rejected any traumatic aftereffects of external stressors.

After eight days, an email from Dr. Forsbach arrives: "Yes, we all speak [about] the same person, Friedrich Panse. Your enclosed document comes from him." He added that it is a well-known scandal among historians of psychiatry that Panse continued to teach as a professor after the war, and that he continued to review cases of people affected by Nazi crimes.[1]

"A well-known scandal," but in 1964, when they waited impatiently for the expert opinion, I don't think my mom or any of her partners to this claim had any idea whom they were dealing with because they primarily complained about the delays in getting his report. That year, nothing happened in the case. Lucie started taking

French lessons, and my mom started taking driving lessons (hoping to buy a car one day). After some months of silence, a letter was sent: What is taking so long?[2] But the expert was silent, and folder number 1238 was gathering dust. Only in March 1965, the *Scheiße* hit the fan when the expert opinion from Dr. Panse arrived in Tel Aviv: Consistent with his general outlook, he stated that it does not seem likely that a causal link existed between the events of 1933 and the suicide. When considering the picture, he claims it is likely that this is part of the depression of the elderly (which is often linked to cerebral sclerosis). The depression, in this case, started more than 20 years after the immigration, and it looks like an endogenous disease. In other words, it is not attributable to external factors.[3]

41 TEL AVIV

"I CAN'T GO ON."

How oblivious I was of her pain. All I was thinking of at the time were silly tricks and pranks. Once, when Eva and I discovered that our nerdy mom had never been inside a sleeping bag, we convinced her to try. We got her to lie on the floor in the "hall," persuading her to slide into the tight bag while keeping her hands beside her body. Then we pulled the zipper all the way up, sat on the armchair by the phone, and listened to the mummy begging us: "Let me out." Of course, I don't think I had ever seen her happier than when she was alternating between protesting and laughing on the floor. It was one of our happiest moments as a family, almost like the times we would listen together to *West Side Story* or *My Fair Lady* on Saturday mornings. Yet now that I think about it, it was around that time that I also told her that joke that falling from a tall building won't kill you. I cringe as I think about my mom and can feel the icy stare that would appear on her face when she was angry. Mom, I didn't know. If I had a time machine, I would zip back to 1965 and report to you everything I now know about Dr. Panse instead of telling you stupid jokes.

Dr. Panse's report arrived in Tel Aviv on Thursday, March 11, 1965, which was exactly a week before Purim, and I was probably bugging my mom about my Purim costume while she was thinking that she's had it. But she was quickly back at her typewriter, and by Saturday, she'd finished typing a new statement that asserted that her dad's condition didn't just suddenly start 20 years after he'd arrived in Palestine, as the expert assumes, but had started much earlier. "I don't know if my dad was a joyful person before he immigrated to Palestine, but as long as I remember him here, he suffered from depression," she wrote. To support her claim, she got affidavits from two people who had known him in his early years in Tel Aviv: Else Schweitzer and Arthur Katz. Schweitzer wrote about their long-term acquaintances with the Mendels as neighbors from the very first months in Tel Aviv. "Doctor Mendel never took root in Palestine," she wrote. "He was very attached to his previous line of work, and in all the years I had known him, he never overcame the fact that he had been torn away from his profession." She remembered how he used to tell her and her husband: *Ich habe es satt* (I'm fed up), and *Ich kann das nicht mehr mitmachen* ("I can't go on") and how she and her husband would encourage him to remove thoughts of suicide. Arthur Katz, who was now working in a shoe store in New York, remembered how Hugo would tell him about the huge difference between his life in Germany and his life in Palestine. "Hugo didn't speak Hebrew and never felt at home in Israel," Katz wrote. "I was under the impression that he missed Germany greatly but that after so many years and everything that had happened, he would not find his place there."[1]

Dr. Lichtenstein wrote a long letter to Dahlfeld to express his disappointment in the expert. They'd been waiting for so long for his opinion, and what finally arrived didn't make sense and was not scientifically based.[2] Dahlfeld sent the court a document of his own. He said that the expert opinion demonstrates that it's impossible to answer the question using only a psychiatric perspective. He cited from a list that had been compiled and published of Jewish attorneys who had committed suicide as a result of Nazi persecution, including Dr. Georg Pick from Berlin, Dr. Jakob Bär who'd poisoned himself, Dr. Friedrich Schöndorf from Breslau, and Dr. Adolf Friedlaender from Limburg. And he added names of lawyers who'd ended their lives together with their wives, including Karl Neumeyer from Munich, Guido Leser from Heidelberg, and Richard Kann from Berlin. All these cases occurred under the Nazi regime, and Dahlfeld's point was clear. It was the persecution and not some internal depression that led to their deaths. Is it so difficult to believe that the persecution and what followed would cause someone to commit suicide two decades later? Especially because the deceased had just returned from a visit to Germany where he realized so painfully how he'd been derailed from his life?[3]

A few weeks after these letters were sent, a new hope emerged from an unexpected place. My mom, Lichtenstein, and Dahlfeld had been following for some time the case of Dr. Wolfgang Freund in Germany's highest court, BGH. Freund was a Jewish pharmacist who had escaped to Shanghai during Nazi times. After the war, he moved to Australia with his wife and daughter, and once he found out that his parents and other family members had died in Europe, he became deeply depressed and killed himself in 1954. His wife and daughter demanded restitution, but the German authorities refused. Yet in February 1965, the BGH determined that it's reasonable to believe that the persecution lowered Freund's psychological resilience, and therefore, those who had persecuted him were responsible for his death. After the court meeting in May 1965, Dahlfeld sent an encouraging note: The judges said that the decision in Freund's case created a completely new picture and suggested that the case would go back to the LRB to see whether it could pay without continuing the court trial.[4] Both sides agreed, yet a few months later, the LRB came back and rejected the demand again. It sees no reason to change the previous decision, the LRB argued. The next court meeting was scheduled for March 28, 1966, but a couple of days before the meeting, the presiding judge called Dahlfeld with an awkward request. Most of the documents in the file had disappeared. Can we postpone the meeting?

Disappeared?

Yes, the file itself is here, but it contains only a few pages. The judge assumes that the rest of the documents fell out of the folder and are somewhere around the court. The court staff had looked everywhere but so far haven't found them. Can the meeting be postponed? Dahlfeld refused.[5] At the meeting, the court had expressed its disappointment that the LRB insisted on continuing through the legal route. Dahlfeld asked that the court expedites the efforts to search for the lost documents because of Lucie's advanced age.

* * *

If there was one thing that drove my mom and Oma nuts, it was clutter, and this is where I recall the most friction I had with them as a child. When Oma saw something that wasn't supposed to be on the floor in my room, she would lean against the door frame and focus her gaze on the object as if she were trying to elevate it with her telekinetic power until I'd give up and return it myself to the shelf. Chaos in my room would also awaken Onkel Max's bad temper in my mom with an occasional *"Scheiße!"* or even a *"Verdammte Scheiße!"* So from my personal experience, the clerks at that court were lucky my mom and Oma didn't fly directly to Düsseldorf. I'm sure Oma and my mom were shocked that this could happen in Germany. In one of the court sessions a few months earlier, the LRB representative showed up without the file and could not answer any questions because the material wasn't in front of him.[6] Oma and my mother never got used to the Israeli *balagan* (chaos), but in Germany?

A few weeks later, a letter from Dahlfeld arrived with good news: The documents had been found! It turned out they'd been placed in the folder of one Alfred Mendel. "I cannot decide if this was an innocent mistake or not," Dahlfeld wrote.[7] I can hear the irritation in her voice as I read my mom's letter to Dahlfeld: "Mrs. Mendel doesn't know anyone by the name of Alfred Mendel. Alfred

Mendel's case has nothing to do with Lucie Mendel. We ask that you verify that all the documents are completely separated again."[8]

It seemed that everything was working against them. Around that time, Dr. Friedrich Panse was elected president of the German Society for Psychiatry and Neurology.[9] Yes, the man who recommended the murder of patients with mental illness was elected by his peers to head the organization that is supposed to help such patients. But then, in the darkness, a beam of hope emerged in Lucie Mendel's lawsuit. In September 1966, despite Panse's high status and in direct contradiction of his opinion, the court stated unequivocally that Hugo Mendel's suicide was caused by the persecution and encouraged the sides to reach an agreement.[10] When the LRB refused to change its position, the court convened to announce its decision. On March 6, 1967, the court reiterated its position that Hugo Mendel had suffered from depression resulting from uprooting (known in German as *Entwurzelungsdepression*) and announced that the state would have to pay Mrs. Mendel a monthly pension (and retroactively from Hugo Mendel's death which added up to 78,367 German marks). Dr. Lichtenstein admitted that he was surprised because courts tend to accept expert opinions in such cases. Dahlfeld was quick to point out that the other party might still appeal. On the other hand, he mused, maybe the LRB just needed someone to decide for it and would now leave this case alone.[11]

42 TEL AVIV
"ESPECIALLY WHEN THEY'RE ASLEEP."

In May 1967, some kids at school said that Hitler might finally accomplish what he had planned all along. We heard about Egyptian tanks at the border, ready to attack, and that they might wipe us out. The men of the neighborhood had been at the front for weeks. Levi Eshkol, the prime minister, was seen as weak and didn't instill a great deal of confidence. The neighborhood had no bomb shelters, and the possibility of shelling was real because our house was less than ten miles from the border with the West Bank, at that time, Jordanian territory. So we kids dug trenches in the backyards, partly excited and partly scared. At the end of May, Levi Eshkol gave a speech on the radio, and he stumbled on some words, making people even more worried. Is this the guy who's going to lead us to victory? On June 1, Moshe Dayan, a former chief of staff of the IDF, became the minister of defense, and everyone said that things should be better now.

Eva and I volunteered to dig trenches all around the neighborhood, and when the time came to dig one in our backyard, we were so tired that we stopped midway. When my mom returned home that day, she took a look at the shallow trench and muttered, "Charity begins at home." That night, when the sirens were heard, she told us to get under her bed in the front room, and as the three of us were lying there, we started hearing loud explosions. The following day, I went to see a house that was hit, not far from ours. The whole front of the house was gone, and you could see into the family's apartment as if it were a dollhouse. Luckily, the family that lived there was in their trench. The kids said that the Jordanians were aiming for Moshe Dayan's house, in our neighborhood, but that they missed. In a couple of days, things turned around dramatically, and Israel captured Sinai, the West Bank, and the Golan Heights. My mom looked happy but not as happy as everyone else around did. She was part of everything, and unlike her father, she felt she belonged in Israel, but always a bit from the sidelines. My cousin Techia, who was left with two young children after her husband was killed in that war, came one evening to talk to my mom. They spoke for a long time in the living room, and when they were done, my mom called me to the room and said to Techia, "You see? They grow up to be good kids." Two-second pause. "Especially when they're asleep," she added, and she caressed my cheek with the back of her hand.

About a month after the Six Day War, the LRB fired back by filing an appeal against Lucie Mendel. How could the judges ignore the opinion of a renowned medical expert such as Dr. Panse and make their own diagnosis that the depression had resulted from uprooting?[1] Dahlfeld responded that if the other party were to question the court authority to determine what had happened, this would amount to "medical arrogance."[2] On a different matter, the LRB blamed the court for accepting Mrs. Mendel's financial statement without checking it too carefully. How did her capital decrease so much in 1964 and 1965? The LRB asked and stated it assumed Mrs. Mendel had invested her money somewhere without reporting it to the court.

Dr. Lichtenstein was in Europe at the time where (among other things) he was meeting with Günter Grass who had become interested in the Jews of Danzig, his birthplace, for his book *From the Diary of a Snail*.[3] But after such accusations from the LRB, my mom couldn't wait for her boss to return. There was no bigger offense than to doubt my mom's integrity, and she had to respond. Dr. Lichtenstein would address the other points, she wrote to Dahlfeld, but for now, she would explain the numbers. There is no inconsistency. Mrs. Mendel's capital decreased in 1964 because she had spent some money in the previous year to finance some activities, including a trip to Europe for her daughter.[4]

In December 1967, Dahlfeld reported that the high court had decided to assign a new expert: Dr. Walter Ritter von Baeyer, a psychiatrist and professor at Heidelberg who had co-authored a book about the psychology of the persecuted.[5] Von Baeyer may have looked promising, but Dr. Lichtenstein and my mom could not hide their deep disappointment. They were hoping that the court would reject the LRB's appeal, but now things had started all over again, including the long waits for news and letters asking what was taking so long.[6] In October 1968, Dahlfeld sent the court a reminder: Mrs. Mendel would celebrate her 70th birthday the following month.[7]

43 TEL AVIV

"IN GOOD AND BAD TIMES, SHE ALWAYS REMAINED BRAVE."

I'm standing in front of Dr. Lichtenstein's office at 13 Yosef Eliyahu Street in Tel Aviv. In 1967, the tall man was ready to retire, so he moved all the files from Allenby 112 to a converted garage in the apartment building where he lived. He was hoping to start closing cases and to focus on other things such as documenting the history of the Jews of Danzig. It is a short and narrow street in the middle of the city, and even though it's around noon, no car has driven by here in the past ten minutes. Just a few houses down the street lived Menachem Begin (the former prime minister of Israel) who had said that restitution money was stained with blood and vehemently fought against accepting any money from Germany, and here in this small office, several hundred files of the Jews of Danzig were cramped along with file number 1238 of Lucie Mendel from Hamm. Yet despite Dr. Lichtenstein's plans to start closing files, the cases refused to close. In this tiny room with its strong scent of cardboard, Dr. Lichtenstein, my mother, another secretary, and one or two clients would crowd together for another 20 years. A tiny square was closed off at the corner of the room and served as a bathroom, and when a client would turn to it (some came from Haifa or Jerusalem), my mother would start typing in an especially energetic staccato to cover any sounds that might come from there.

I lean against a parked car and look at the office and remember how she would tell me about the budding friendship between Dr. Lichtenstein and Günter Grass and how she had labored for days cleaning up this cave and arranging the cardboard files as much as possible for Grass's visit to the office. (This was years before he'd won the Nobel Prize for Literature and even more years before he'd admitted that he had joined a Waffen-SS unit at the age of 17.) I also remember what my mom wrote about her first visit to Germany: "When I was standing in Munich before the court building where my father had appeared several times, I was gripped by rage against those who had expelled him from his profession, his homeland, his cultural and spiritual surroundings, and are responsible for his death." And I miss this woman who fought so stubbornly for her father and mother.

Indeed, as Dahlfeld had advised the court, Oma celebrated her 70th birthday in November 1968, and in the weeks leading to the event, my mom was spending some extra time at her typewriter. The lines she was typing were shorter now, and the smoking breaks were longer than usual. We had a tradition of writing poems for birthdays, and my mom was laboring over a song of praise to her mom. Writers of those hymns would usually focus on finding rhymes and good laughs from the audience (and my mom too used the opportunity to suggest that maybe she would spend some time in Paris and that "the boy" (her brother Raphi) would explain to Oma the postal strikes in France.) But she also allowed herself to include a serious verse in the song: 70 years ago, the world wasn't crazy yet, but since then, man had made sure to change that. Lucie knew some beautiful times, but also hard times, and these did not pass without leaving their traces. Yet one thing cannot be denied: In good and bad times, she always remained brave.

Many months passed with back-and-forth correspondence. Dahlfeld suggested another expert because the professor was slow to submit his report. The judges rejected this suggestion but, after a while, sent Professor von Baeyer an impatient letter. When his report arrived, it turned out that von Baeyer completely disagreed with Panse, the previous expert. Indeed, von Baeyer wrote, this was a case of depression resulting from uprooting that was augmented by reactive depression and worsened by cerebral sclerosis.[1]

It seems that the new report raised anger at the LRB, which wondered what exactly made von Baeyer better than Dr. Panse, and Dahlfeld responded that it was his experience that made him better. Von Baeyer specialized in the psychology of persecution, and therefore, he could point out a case of depression that resulted from uprooting when he saw one. The LRB presented a document from one of its own physicians questioning von Baeyer's theory. Cerebral sclerosis that supposedly worsened the case was never proven by a heart attack or a stroke. And why did the court base its decision on testimonies of family members or non-professionals such as Schweitzer or Arthur Katz? And was it a suicide, or was it an accident as the family had claimed right after Dr. Mendel's death?

"Merde!"

And then, one day in November 1969, seven years and five months after Lucie Mendel had sent her initial claim, the final ruling of the court arrived. In a long document, the judges patiently explained their decision point by point, like wise tribe elders who have seen it all. True, there seems to be a contradiction between the accident and the suicide versions, but it is well-known that families often try to cover the suicide of their loved ones for societal reasons. The court does not doubt that this was a suicide. Regarding the claim that the court accepts the testimony of non-professionals to determine the depression, the judges explained that in numerous cases they get from psychiatrists, these professionals themselves rely on the testimonies of friends and family members. The court trusts the witnesses and sees no reason not to believe them. With empathy and compassion, the judges wrote about their colleague, Dr. Hugo Mendel, who came back to his homeland in 1956 where he realized that not only this was no longer his homeland, but also that he was no longer the man who had left it 23 years earlier.

Whoever caused him to leave the country in the first place was responsible for his death, the court determined. The state of North Rhine-Westphalia must pay Lucie Mendel the sum that had been previously determined. [2]

The day my mom got the news about the win, she had to be careful. If she did a victory lap around the house, we might ask too many questions, and she would need to tell us about her father's suicide (which she had avoided all these years). I remember that she told us something about Oma receiving a great deal of money because the Germans had destroyed Opa's health. My mom was exhausted, no doubt, but this was the exhaustion of a marathon runner, or more aptly, a lawyer who had just won the biggest case of her life. She ensured that her mom could live the rest of her life in dignity. And perhaps more importantly, the daughter who had sat 40 years earlier by the typewriter in his law office, proved that the Nazis were responsible for the death of her father—and something that Hugo Mendel would have loved—that the court could force the state to accept this truth. Now I understand that the trip my mom, my sister, and I had made to Europe a few months after the trial was such a victory lap, and I'm sure that our visit to Zurich closed a circle in my mom's mind. She did not have the energy or interest in visiting Germany, but she did include the city of her parents' refuge in our trip.

As for myself, I would be lying if I said that I have no anger toward Hugo for abandoning his daughter, for abandoning us. Yet over the years, my anger has subsided some, as I have come to better understand some things. I understood that he saved our family by convincing Lucie to leave Germany in 1933. I understood that we shared our love for his daughter, who was also my mom. And I understood that I don't know much about tortured souls. In her 1943 article "We Refugees," Hannah Arendt wrote about suicide. Religious people, Arendt explained, view suicide, like murder, as "a blasphemous attack on creation as a whole," and a type of declaration that life isn't worth living. Secular European Jews who chose to end their own lives were different; she argued that "...our suicides are no mad rebels who hurl defiance at life and the world, who try to kill in themselves the whole universe. Theirs is a quiet and modest way of vanishing; they seem to apologize for the violent solution they have found for their personal problems."[3] I don't know whether Hugo meant his suicide as a protest to declare that life is not worth living or whether he just wanted to vanish quietly. If the latter was his intention, I'm afraid he didn't disappear quietly, because his suicide screamed in my mother's head her entire life.

I made most of this trip when I was 50, but a voice in me told me, "Come back to this book when you're his age," and today, when I reached the age at which he died, I'm still angry at him, but I also feel surges of compassion. And after going through the thick file, after hearing all the testimonies, and after reading the judges' opinions, the rage I felt when I first saw Opa at my dad's funeral has been replaced mainly by great sadness. Whenever I hear about someone committing suicide, I think of my mom banging on the steering wheel and crying, "Those damn guilty feelings," and I'm sad that she carried those with her for all these years.

EPILOGUE

My mom continued to work for Dr. Lichtenstein for many years, helping survivors receive their restitution money from Germany. She never talked about specific cases, but I know that many people were grateful to her because there was a drawer in the credenza in our living room, where I would often find a box of assorted chocolates, and when I would ask her where she had gotten it, she would say:

"It's from a client. She suddenly showed up at the office with this."

When Dr. Lichtenstein decided to cut the cord and retire (after years in that converted garage), he appealed to the Israeli Ministry of Justice to pass his business to my mom even though she didn't have a law degree. The issue went all the way to the Minister of Justice, but he did not approve it.[1] I think my mom was greatly relieved because she was ready to retire too. The truth is that for several years, she went to work only out of loyalty to him and their clients. She would dress up in the morning, utter something about "this lousy office," glance at the little sign in the "hall" that she'd bought on one of her trips and read, "Today is the first day of the rest of your life," and would then rush to work. Now that he was retiring, and she could not take on the business, she was looking forward to some quiet time of reading, traveling, and spending time with her grandchildren. She also started auditing classes at Tel Aviv University in linguistics, translation, and history. "Maybe I'll make something of myself after all," she wrote to me.

* * *

In 1972, a year before the psychiatrist Friedrich Panse died, the German Society for Psychiatry and Neurology awarded him honorary membership, but in 2011, the society revoked his honorary membership, arguing that his "involvement in selecting euthanasia victims" constituted a "complicity in genocide."[2]

* * *

"Where is our home? Where we are born or where we wish to die?" This is how the playwright Carl Zuckmayer opened his autobiography. As a German with Jewish roots (who escaped to the United States and died in Switzerland) he was extremely familiar with this dilemma. When we told my mom that we intended to stay in California, she accepted our decision but encouraged us not to think about it in drastic terms. "Thank God we're not talking about leaving a country one cannot return to (which is the case for those leaving the Soviet Union or was the case for my parents when they left Germany)," she wrote. "I think that these days, one can feel a bit more cosmopolitan, with an option to live in one country or another," she added. "And yet, when I read this morning's paper, and in general think about all the *chara* (shit) here, sadly, I'm for you staying there," she wrote.

Driven by a motherly instinct, she tried to prepare me for the eternal conflict of the immigrant, the conflict she and her father knew so well: "When you are here, you'll miss there in the same way that you now miss what's here." Indeed, I missed Israel, especially in the early years, and I'm connected forever to its music and my friends and family there. "In German, they talk about 'heart fibers' and in English about 'heartstrings,'" my mom wrote to us. She added that even though she had never been too good in anatomy, she was convinced that something like this exists. "It's a fact that something is drawn like strings to you guys: I think about you all the time and want to know everything about your impressions, experiences, and actions." The least I could do was to grant this request, and I wrote my mom a letter every week. On her calls with Oma, she would translate the letters, and Oma would record the latest smart comments of her great-grandchildren so that she could share them with her *Yekke* friends.

Oma never left the small apartment on 5 Reines Street. The trip to Cyprus was the last time she left Israel, but she was perfectly *zufrieden*. She spent her money and her time on the one thing she valued more than anything else: family. Even as an adult, whenever I would visit her, she would reach for her wallet, grab some money, and push a bill into my hand. There was no point in arguing. For her, sitting at a café, facing the sidewalk of course, while watching a grandchild (or a great-grandchild) read a book and laugh—this was the essence of the good life. As for sugar packets, she didn't stop stealing those to her last day.

In 1986, Oma suffered a stroke and was rushed to the hospital where she stayed for many months. During that time, the *ganovim* (thieves) finally broke into the apartment, but my mom, who knew that with her luck this was bound to happen, had already cleared out most of the valuables. Oma would cry a lot in the hospital, from sad things or happy things. When my mom came to tell her that we were expecting our fourth child, my mom preceded it with a long discussion with Oma about what is worth crying over and what is not. Following this preparation, when my mom told Oma about the pregnancy, she just laughed.

"I'm so afraid of her crying because I must hold back crying too," my mom wrote.

Oma died in 1988. On her last days, there was one word on her lips, my mom told me. Oma called out for her mom in German: "*Mutti.*"

In 1992, my mom was diagnosed with cancer. Dr. Lichtenstein was still alive, but he could not come to the hospital. I brought a letter from him to her room in the intensive care unit, and she read it to me aloud. Twice in my life had my mom burst into tears when reading me a letter. This was the second occasion. The first time was when I asked her to translate a letter that the leaders of the Jewish community of Hamm had sent to her father before the family left for Tel Aviv in 1933. Her voice started trembling when she reached the paragraph in which they thanked him for his volunteer work in the community, which he performed with so much love and competence. She broke down in the next paragraph: "We hope and wish that you may soon have better prospects for the future, and we look forward to hearing from you soon that you have been compensated for all the anguish that you and your family have suffered through no fault of your own in recent months."

My mom got out of intensive care and was going to be released from the hospital the following day. I had to return to Berkeley, and it was time to say good-bye. I hugged her in the hospital corridor, and she bit her pinky not to cry. I kissed her and walked away. She cried in her room, and I cried in the stairwell. After a few days in Berkeley, I had to see her one more time, and just as with the glass door that I kept open at the *Kurhaus* in Wiesbaden to remember the garden, I flew back to Israel to be with her during her last days. On September 20, 1992, I stood at the bottom of the escalator, and I watched her going up, waving good-bye.

* * *

I still hear random words in German in my head whenever I visit Germany, but I have become used to them, and they are not as frenzied as on that first visit to Düsseldorf. My relationships with Germany have evolved over the years; while I mostly felt like a complete stranger on my first visits, I feel a bit more at home now. Of course, the shift in my feelings didn't occur overnight, but if I had to pick a turning point, I would focus on one late afternoon in December 2003.

The city of Hamm erected a memorial in the parking lot where the synagogue used to stand, and I was invited to attend the dedication. I wasn't looking forward to it, because I don't get particularly excited by ceremonies that are typically attended by a few dignitaries and guests of honor. But I decided to go anyway.

The ceremony was planned for 4 p.m. It was a cold and gloomy day, and I was sure that nobody (beyond those who had to be there) would show up. Indeed, as I expected, the area around the parking lot was nearly empty when I arrived. The mayor and his team greeted us, a few descendants of Jewish families from Hamm. A television crew arrived and interviewed my uncle Raphi and Paul Otto Samuelsdorff. I stood there for a long time staring at the small stage where the last preparations were taking place. A technician checked whether the microphone worked. Some high school students (maybe a choir?) were hanging out by the stage. A man wearing a *kippah* (a rabbi or cantor?) was going through some papers. It was already a bit darker, and then I turned around and saw them—the people of Hamm: men and women, tall and short, skinny and plump—I had been fixated on that stage for so long that I had paid no attention to what had been going on behind my back. They stood along the sidewalk quietly, and more people were joining them. They didn't cross the line between the sidewalk and the parking lot where we were standing, as if they were an honor guard that was there to pay respect, to close a circle. It wasn't a small crowd, maybe two or three hundred people—enough to show that this was beyond an administrative act of remembrance. And when the mayor approached the microphone and began talking, the people of Hamm crossed the line into the parking lot and stood around us, with us.

Since that time, I have visited Hamm on several occasions. On one recent visit, Mechtild Brand took me to a refugee shelter that she and a group of friends had started not far from Hamm to accommodate several dozen asylum seekers from Syria, Sudan, Eritrea, and other countries. It was a bright day in March, the grass was green, and children were laughing in the distance, and when we walked toward one of the buildings, Mechtild pointed my attention to some shutters that were completely rolled down.

"Look at these windows," she said. "People get depressed."

It was ten in the morning, and Mechtild explained that some of the residents who can't find jobs were still asleep. My grandfather Hugo came to my mind in that small apartment in Tel Aviv. I had never thought about it before, but I bet that as he was sitting for hours in bed in his buttoned-up pajamas, the shutters were rolled down all the way too.

And I remember how when I would sleep over at Oma's apartment, she would come into the room in the morning and briskly pull up the shutters all the way, and the light would flood the room.

ILLUSTRATIONS

The following list describes the photos appearing under the title of each chapter. All photos are from the author's collection unless specified otherwise.

1. **Tel Aviv.** Mirjam Rosen looking through the kitchen window. 1960s.

2. **Menlo Park.** The box of letters Hugo and Lucie Mendel sent from their 1956 trip.

3. **Los Angeles.** Martin Mendel at his house in Los Angeles, 2010.

4. **New York.** Gertrud Katz at her apartment in New York. 2003.

5. **Above the Ocean.** Flight map.

6. **Tel Aviv.** Hugo and Lucie Mendel, circa 1940s.

7. **Tel Aviv.** The author holding Hugo's camera, June 1957.

8. **Tel Aviv.** The author and his sister on Purim 1956.

9. **Tel Aviv.** Mirjam Rosen, Eva, and Emanuel, circa 1963.

10. **Tel Aviv.** Yehuda Rosen's funeral, October 1953.

11. **Munich.** Part of a Swissair postcard found at Lucie Mendel's apartment.

12. **Amsterdam.** A page from Hugo Mendel's Israeli passport. Stamp of the Dutch Consulate in Tel Aviv and of the border control in Amsterdam.

13. **Düsseldorf.** A Hugo Boss shopping bag at Lindenhof Hotel. September 2003.

14. **Düsseldorf.** A postcard sent to the author by his grandparents, featuring the hedgehogs from the Mecki series. Published courtesy of Anton Diehl.

15. **Düsseldorf.** Hugo Mendel with other Jewish students at the University of Bonn around the year 1915. Published courtesy of the Central Zionist Archive in Jerusalem. PHG/1007429. I first detected the picture in S. Poppel, *Zionism in Germany 1897– 1933* (Philadelphia: Jewish Publication Society of America, 1977).

16. **Wiesbaden.** Lucie Mendel, Liese Mendel (later Rawitz), and Mirjam Mendel (later Rosen). Taken by Hugo Mendel in Wiesbaden 1925.

17. **Wiesbaden.** Hugo Mendel, circa 1931.

18. **Wiesbaden.** Lucie Mendel with daughter, Mirjam, and son, Raphi at Café Mendel, circa 1935.

19. **Wiesbaden.** Hugo Mendel with daughter, Mirjam, 1925, Wiesbaden.

20. **Frankfurt.** Mary and Franz Fürstenberg, 1958.

21. **Wiesbaden.** Stairs at Hotel Bären in Wiesbaden.

22. **Düsseldorf.** The picture features Düsseldorf's famous tradition of kids cartwheeling. Düsseldorfer Radschläger auf dem Burgplatz um 1900. Wikimedia Commons / Public Domain.

23. **Hamm.** Paul Otto Samuelsdorff near his family home in Hamm, September 2003.

24. **Menden.** Martin Mendel in Menden with two daughters of the Stracke family, 1946.

25. **Northeim.** Nettchen Stern, Lucie Mendel, and Raphi Medan in Tel Aviv, 1935 or 1936.

26. **Hannover.** The train station in Linden Hannover.

27. **Riga.** The Šķirotava train station in Riga.

28. **Düsseldorf.** The entrance to the Apollo Theater in Düsseldorf.

29. **"Düsseldorf isn't what it used to be."** Düsseldorf's famous Fountain of Youth. Märchenbrunnen (Jugendbrunnen), 1904-1905, Max Blondat. © Micha L. Rieser

30. **Zurich.** *Bahnhofstraße* in Zurich. Istock.com/Denis Linine.

31. **Rapperswil.** Part of a postcard Hugo and Lucie sent featuring their hotel in Rapperswil.

32. **Tel Aviv.** Eva Dimand (née Rosen) as a ballerina on Purim 1957.

33. **Tel Aviv.** Hugo Mendel's obituary notice in the German newspaper published in Tel Aviv.

34. **Tel Aviv.** Eva Dimand (née Rosen) and Emanuel Rosen on Purim 1958.

35. **Jerusalem.** Raphi Medan as a young man.

36. **Nicosia.** Nicosia, Cyprus. Istock.com/Kirillm.

37. **Tel Aviv.** Mirjam Rosen typing at home in summer 1957.

38. **Zurich.** Mirjam Rosen and Sarah Yellin in Europe, 1963.

39. **Tel Aviv.** A document from *Lucie Mendel vs. the State of North Rhine-Westphalia.*

40. **Menlo Park.** Part of the last page of the expert opinion by Dr. Panse.

41. **Tel Aviv.** The author (and his sister's legs).

42. **Tel Aviv.** A house hit by a shell in Neve Mishkan. June 1967.

43. **Tel Aviv.** Dr. Erwin Lichtenstein and Mirjam Rosen outside the office, circa 1968.

Epilogue: Lucie Mendel and Mirjam Rosen, circa 1975. The picture at the end of the Epilogue features Hugo, Lucie, and Mirjam, circa 1925.

Map: iStock/Evgenii Bobrov. Cities added by the author.

Author photo: Hagop's Photography.

PEOPLE IN ALPHABETICAL ORDER

All cities are in Germany, unless noted otherwise.

Besser, Alexander: 1899 (Forst/Lausitz) – 1978 (Offenbach). A German Jewish lawyer who practiced law in Berlin before the war, left for Tel Aviv in 1938, returned to Germany in 1950, and practiced law in Frankfurt for the rest of his life.

Binheim, Harry: 1885 (Duingen) – 1948 (Tel Shalom, Israel). A German Jewish lawyer who practiced law in Hamelin. Immigrated to Tel Aviv in 1938. Husband of Käthe Binheim.

Binheim, Hermann (Zvi): 1919 (Hamelin) –1996 (Karkur, Israel). Son of Harry and Käthe Binheim. Studied agriculture at the Ahlem School of Agriculture. Immigrated to Tel Aviv in 1939.

Binheim Käthe (née Stern): 1895 (Northeim) – 1978 (Karkur, Israel): Sister of Lucie Mendel. Immigrated to Tel Aviv in 1938.

Bödeker, Emmy: Owner of Hotel Bären in Wiesbaden.

Bödeker-Kenke, Beate: Owner of Hotel Bären in Wiesbaden.

Brand, Mechtild: An author of a book about the Jews of Hamm.

Dimand, Eva (née Rosen): 1950 (Tel Aviv). The author's sister. Granddaughter of Hugo and Lucie Mendel.

Dahlfeld, Gert: A lawyer from Duisburg, Germany, who represented Lucie Mendel in her lawsuit against the state of North Rhine-Westphalia.

Fürstenberg, Franz: 1897 (Trier) – 1976 (Freiburg im Breisgau). Left for Manila, Philippines, in 1938. Returned to Germany and lived in Frankfurt during the Mendels' visit. Husband of Mary Fürstenberg.

Fürstenberg, Mary (née Gottschalk): 1902 (Düsseldorf) – 1995 (Freiburg im Breisgau (ca.)). Left for Manila, Philippines, in 1938. Returned to Germany and lived in Frankfurt during the Mendels' visit. Cousin of Hugo Mendel.

Gidion, Robert: 1891–1967. A German Jewish lawyer from Cologne, immigrated to Tel Aviv in 1933, and practiced law there. Served as liquidator of Hugo Mendel's company.

Green, Judith: (née Mendel): 1929 (Iserlohn) – 2003 (Michigan). Martin Mendel's sister.

Grossman, Benjamin: 1914 (Poland) – 2010 (Tel Aviv). Ruth Grossman's husband.

Grossman, Ruth (née Binheim): 1924 (Hameln). Daughter of Harry and Käthe Binheim. Cousin of Mirjam Rosen.

Herzfeld, Hedwig, "Hepps" (née Eichenberg): 1891 (Göttingen) – 1972 (Berlin). Lucie Mendel's cousin.

Herzfeld, Manfred: 1887 (Hannover) – 1968 (Berlin). A German Jewish lawyer who practiced law in Celle before the war. Immigrated to Palestine in 1935. Returned to Germany in 1950 and worked for the JRSO in Berlin. Hedwig Herzfeld's husband.

Katz, Arthur: 1908 (Bochum) –1974 (New York). Cousin of Hugo Mendel.

Katz, Gertrud: 1913 (Nieder-Ohmen) – 2005 (New York). Wife of Arthur Katz.

Katzenstein, Ernst: 1897 (Bodenwerder) – 1989 (Israel). A German Jewish lawyer from Hamelin. Immigrated to Palestine in 1935 and practiced law there. Worked for the JRSO after the war. In 1956, became the director of the Claims Conference in Germany.

Katzenstein, Hilde: Wife of Ernst Katzenstein.

Kieserling, Friedrich: German lawyer from Hamm who represented Hugo Mendel. President of the Hamm Bar Association from 1929 until April 18, 1933, and from 1945 until 1959.

Kugelmann, Hermann: 1891(Witzenhausen) – 1975 (Kassel). A German Jewish lawyer. Worked in Tel Aviv and in Kassel.

Leven, Amalie (Malchen) (née Eichengrün): 1875 (Madfeld, Kr. Brilon) – 1958 (Los Angeles). Grandmother of Martin Mendel.

Leven, Salomon (Sally): 1874 (Krefeld) –1963 (Los Angeles). Grandfather of Martin Mendel.

Lichtenstein, Erwin: 1901 (Königsberg) – 1993 (Tel Aviv). A German Jewish lawyer. After 1933, became the head of the Jewish Community in Danzig and then immigrated to Tel Aviv where he practiced law. Employer of Mirjam Rosen.

Lowenberg, Shlomo (Helmuth): 1919 (Hamborn) – 1991 (Israel). Immigrated to Israel in 1935. Studied law in England. Israeli judge. Lucie and Hugo met him on the flight from Tel Aviv to Munich.

Medan, Raphi: 1926 (Hamm) – 2017 (Mevaseret Zion, Israel). Son of Hugo and Lucie Mendel. Immigrated to Palestine in 1933. Worked for the Israeli Mossad.

Mendel, Else (née Leven): 1901 (Menden) – 1985 (Los Angeles). Wife of Ernst Mendel. Mother of Martin Mendel.

Mendel, Emanuel: 1851 (Coesfeld) – 1921 (Menden). Father of Hugo, Ernst, and Liese Mendel.

Mendel, Emilie (née Samson): 1861 (probably Menden) – 1904 (Unna). Mother of Hugo, Ernst, and Liese Mendel.

Mendel, Ernst: 1893 (Unna) – 1953 (Los Angeles). Hugo Mendel's brother. Martin Mendel's father.

Mendel, Hugo: 1891 (Unna) – 1957 (Tel Aviv). Son of Emilie and Emanuel Mendel. Husband of Lucie Mendel.

Mendel, Judith: See Green, Judith.

Mendel, Liese: See Rawitz, Liese.

Mendel, Lucie (née Stern): 1898 (Northeim) – 1988 (Tel Aviv). Daughter of Louis and Nettchen Stern. Mirjam Rosen's mother.

Mendel, Ludwig: See Medan, Raphi.

Mendel, Martin: 1925 (Iserlohn) – 2011 (Los Angeles). Son of Ernst and Else Mendel.

Rawitz, Liese (Née Mendel). 1895 (Unna) – 1974 (Ramat Gan, Israel). Hugo Mendel's sister. "Tante Liese."

Rose, Franz: Author of a book about the Jews of Menden.

Rosen, Avraham (Menda): 1924 (Zduńska Wola, Poland) – 2010 (Tel Aviv). Yehuda Rosen's brother.

Rosen, Emanuel: 1953 (Tel Aviv). Grandson of Hugo and Lucie Mendel.

Rosen, Eva: See, Dimand, Eva.

Rosen, Mirjam: (Née Mendel). 1922 (Hamm) – 1992 (Tel Aviv). Daughter of Hugo and Lucie Mendel. The author's mother.

Rosen, Yehuda: 1917 (Zduńska Wola, Poland) – 1953 (Tel Aviv). Husband of Mirjam Rosen. The author's father. Financial adviser to the Chief of Staff, Israel Defense Forces.

Rosenberg, Pnina: 1888 (Zduńska Wola, Poland) – 1972 (Tel Aviv). Mother of Yehuda Rosen.

Samson, Bella (Née Cohen): 1834 (Vreden) – 1918 (Menden). Mother of Emilie Mendel and of Max Samson.

Samson, Max: 1862 (probably Menden) – 1937 (Menden). Son of Bella Samson and brother of Emilie Mendel. "Onkel Max."

Samuelsdorff, Erich. 1883 (Wattenscheid) – 1954 (Hamm). A German Jewish lawyer who practiced law in Hamm until 1933. Immigrated in 1936 to Tel Aviv. Returned to Hamm in 1954.

Samuelsdorff, Paul Otto. 1923 (Hamm) – 2020 (Cologne). Immigrated in 1936 to Tel Aviv. Returned to Germany in 1956. Son of Erich Samuelsdorff.

Stern, Louis: 1861 (Lindau) – 1924 (Northeim). Father of Lucie Mendel and Käthe Binheim.

Stern, Nettchen (Née **Kron**): 1871 (Wolfhagen) – 1941/2 (Riga). Mother of Lucie Mendel and Käthe Binheim.

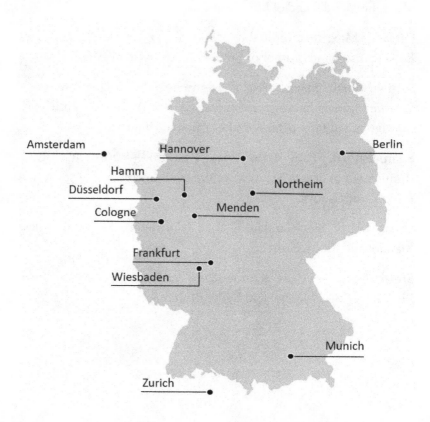

Amsterdam

Hannover

Berlin

Hamm

Northeim

Düsseldorf

Menden

Cologne

Frankfurt

Wiesbaden

Munich

Zurich

Family Members Mentioned in the Book

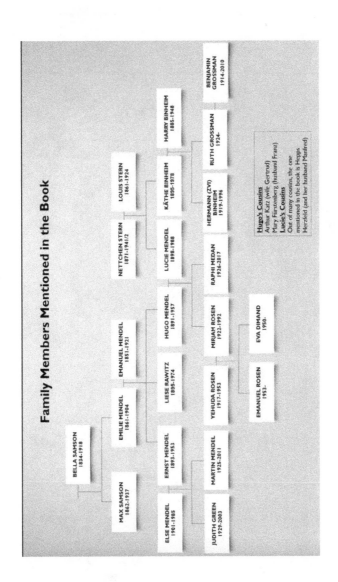

BELLA SAMSON
1834-1918

MAX SAMSON
1862-1937

EMILIE MENDEL
1861-1904

EMANUEL MENDEL
1851-1921

NETTCHEN STERN
1871-1941/2

LOUIS STERN
1861-1924

HARRY BINHEIM
1885-1948

BENJAMIN
GROSSMAN
1914-2010

ELSE MENDEL
1901-1985

ERNST MENDEL
1893-1953

LIESE RAWITZ
1895-1974

HUGO MENDEL
1891-1957

LUCIE MENDEL
1898-1988

KÄTHE BINHEIM
1895-1978

RUTH GROSSMAN
1924-

JUDITH GREEN
1929-2003

MARTIN MENDEL
1925-2011

YEHUDA ROSEN
1917-1953

MIRJAM ROSEN
1922-1992

RAPHI MEDAN
1926-2017

HERMANN (ZVI)
BINHEIM
1919-1996

EMANUEL ROSEN
1953-

EVA DIMAND
1950-

Hugo's Cousins
Arthur Katz (wife Gertrud)
Mary Fürstenberg (husband Franz)
Lucie's Cousins
Out of many cousins, the one
mentioned in the book is Hepps
Herzfeld (and her husband Manfred)

203

NOTES

1. Tel Aviv

1. A general note: This is a true story based on letters, documents, interviews, and my recollection, but in a few places, I took the liberty to modify things. I did not use the real names of Greta S. and Mrs. Steinmann. The journey following my grandparents was not done in one trip and not always in the exact order described in the text. All websites were accessed on December 21, 2020.

2. Menlo Park

1. The letters in the box cover the trip that spanned from August 14, 1956, to October 15, 1956.

3. Los Angeles

1. The Night of Broken Glass. A Nazi-led pogrom against Jews in Germany on 9–10 November 1938.
2. Information about the Fürstenbergs is available in the notes section for chapter 20.
3. Author's multiple interviews and conversations with Martin Mendel. For more information about the Mendel family in Menden, see Franz Rose, *Die Synagogengemeinde Menden 1900–1942* (Menden, 1991).

4. New York

1. Author interview with Gertrud Katz, August 29, 2003.

6. Tel Aviv

1. "Dr. jur. Mendel | lawyer and notary | Hamm (Westphalia) | Große Weststraße 24 I. | phone 967"
2. **Erich Samuelsdorff.** See Mechtild Brand, *Geachtet—geächtet: aus dem Leben Hammer Juden in diesem Jahrhundert* (Hamm: Stadt Hamm, 1991) pp. 129–136. Author interview with Paul Otto Samuelsdorff on June 21, 2003. Author interview with Daniela Samuelsdorff in September 2005. **Hermann Kugelmann.** Author interview with his niece, Idith Althausen, October 16,

2005. His name is mentioned in *Anwalt ohne Recht: Schicksale jüdischer Anwälte in Deutschland nach 1933,* (Bundesrechtsanwaltskammer, be.bra verlag, Berlin, 2007). p. 341. For sources regarding the other lawyers mentioned here (Herzfeld and Katzenstein), see the notes section for chapter 20.

3. For more about the fate of Jewish lawyers in Germany, see Ladwig-Winters, Simone, Lawyers Without Rights: The Fate of Jewish Lawyers in Berlin after 1933 (Washington, D.C.: ABA Publishing, 2018).

10. Tel Aviv

1. About the range of feelings experienced by family members, see: Carla Fine, *No Time to Say Goodbye: Surviving The Suicide of a Loved One* (New York: Broadway Books, 1997).

11. Munich

1. About judge Lowenberg: see *Biographisches Handbuch der deutschsprachigen Emigration nach 1933,* München; New York: K.G. Saur, 1980. Volume I, p. 462.

12. Amsterdam

1. Hugo Mendel received his PhD in 1918 from the University of Greifswald. The title of the dissertation, which he dedicated to his parents and his grandmother Bella Samson, was: "Contributions to the Teaching of Heritable Building Rights."

2. About the Lloyd Hotel before World War II, see M. Felder, C. Minca, and C. E. Ong. "Governing refugee space: The quasi-carceral regime of Amsterdam's Lloyd Hotel, a German-Jewish refugee camp in the prelude to World War II", Geogr. Helv., 69, 365–375, 2014. Available at https://www.geogr-helv.net/69/365/2014/.

13. Düsseldorf

1. The austerity period in Israel took place from 1949 to 1959 and included rationing of food. For more about it see: https://en.wikipedia.org/wiki/Austerity_in_Israel.

14. Düsseldorf

1. For information about Friedrich Panse, refer to the notes section for chapter 40.

2. Multiple interviews and email exchanges with Mechtild Brand.

15. Düsseldorf

1. Another small example of Hugo's Zionism: On the occasion of his engagement to Lucie Mendel, he donated money to plant ten trees in Palestine through the Jewish National Fund. See also: Mechtild Brand, *Geachtet—geächtet: aus dem Leben Hammer Juden in diesem Jahrhundert* (Hamm: Stadt Hamm, 1991) p. 116.

16. Wiesbaden

1. Interview with Emmy Bödeker and with Beate Bödeker-Kenke, September 9, 2003.

17. Wiesbaden

1. About the Neroberg car: https://en.wikipedia.org/wiki/Nerobergbahn.

18. Wiesbaden

1. Café Mendel existed between 1934 and 1938. It was then opened by new owners as Café Ofek.

20. Frankfurt

1. **Mary and Franz Fürstenberg.** Author's multiple interviews with Martin Mendel; author interview with Frank Ephraim, October 2003. As a young boy, Ephraim escaped to the Philippines with his parents and knew the Fürstenbergs. For more general information about German Jews in Manila, see: Ephraim, Frank. *Escape to Manila: From Nazi Tyranny to Japanese Terror* (University of Illinois Press, 2003); For birth and death years of the Fürstenbergs, see the Jewish Museum Berlin, Sammlung Familien Wurm / Fürstenberg, https://objekte.jmberlin.de/person/jmb-pers-472065 (Franz) and https://objekte.jmberlin.de/person/jmb-pers-472373 (Mary).
2. **Ernst Katzenstein.** Author interview with Dr. Michael Katzenstein, son of Ernst Katzenstein, June 10, 2004. Regarding Katzenstein's assignment as head of the Claims Conference in Germany, see Jewish Telegraphic Agency, Daily News Bulletin, Thursday March 22, 1956; *Anwalt ohne Recht: Schicksale jüdischer Anwälte in Deutschland nach 1933*, (Bundesrechtsanwaltskammer, be.bra verlag, Berlin, 2007). p. 128; for entry in German Wikipedia, see: https://de.wikipedia.org/wiki/Ernst_Katzenstein.
3. **Manfred Herzfeld.** Interviews with Miriam Loewy, his granddaughter, on December 15, 2004, and August 31, 2005. See also Miriam Loewy's short story

about her grandfather (in German): *Wer niest denn da?* http://oxfort.de/
family.htm. The line from Herzfeld's poem about the judges who "turned
justice into a prostitute of politics," is from Manfred Herzfeld, *Gruss An
Deutschland: Eine Abrechnung in Versen* (Jerusalem, 1947) p. 12. The verse from
his poem Deutscher Richter: *Sie haben das Recht zur Dirne / Der Politik gemacht;
/ Sie haben mit eherner Stirne / Der Moloch Opfer gebracht.* About Ilse Herzfeld
(Manfred Herzfeld's sister) and her marriage to William S. Burroughs, see *The
Beats: A Literary Reference*, edited by Matt Theado (Carroll & Graf Publishers,
2003) p. 324.

21. Wiesbaden

1. **Alexander Besser.** Author interview with Hansjörg Schiebe, a lawyer in
   Frankfurt who was Besser's business partner. December 2, 2003. The German
   author Peter Härtling wrote a book about Besser: Härtling, Peter. *Felix
   Guttmann.* (Luchterhand, 1985). In the book itself, Härtling states that Felix
   Guttmann is based on "A.B.," but in later years, he acknowledged that it was
   based on the life of Alexander Besser, his friend. In addition to his work as a
   lawyer, Besser was a journalist who covered Jewish and other issues.
   Regarding Mirjam Rosen's acquaintance with Besser, letter from Mirjam
   Rosen to the author, July 23, 1985.
2. Harry Binheim's name appears in *Anwalt ohne Recht: Schicksale jüdischer
   Anwälte in Deutschland nach 1933,* (Bundesrechtsanwaltskammer, be.bra verlag,
   Berlin, 2007). p. 124.
3. Erich Samuelsdorff's return from Tel Aviv to Hamm in 1954 is described by
   Mechtild Brand, *Geachtet—geächtet: aus dem Leben Hammer Juden in diesem
   Jahrhundert* (Hamm: Stadt Hamm, 1991) pp. 129–136.
4. Erwin Lichtenstein, *Bericht an meine Familie: ein Leben zwischen Danzig und
   Israel* (Darmstadt: Luchterhand, 1985).
5. The expression *Goyim naches* is Yiddish and refers to activities that non-Jews
   may enjoy (but not Jews).

22. Düsseldorf

1. The information regarding Kieserling is based on a lecture given by Mechtild
   Brand on October 10, 1991. Transcript in Hebrew. Translated from German by
   Mirjam Rosen.

23. Hamm

1. Author interview with Paul Otto Samuelsdorff on June 21, 2003, and
   conversations on the visit to Schwefe and Hamm on September 4, 2003.
2. My father died on his birthday according to the Hebrew calendar.
3. The term used by Jews for the anniversary of a person's death.

4. "Dr. jur. Mendel | lawyer and notary | Hamm (Westphalia) | Große Weststraße 24 I. | phone 967".

5. Author interview with Mechtild Brand, September 5, 2003. Mechtild Brand, *Geachtet—geächtet: aus dem Leben Hammer Juden in diesem Jahrhundert* (Hamm: Stadt Hamm, 1991), pp. 112-118.

24. Menden

1. Author's multiple interviews with Martin Mendel. Franz Rose, *Die Synagogengemeinde Menden 1900–1942* (Menden, 1991); USC Shoah Foundation for Visual History and Education. Interview with Martin Mendel, May 17, 1996. Interview Code: 15367.

25. Northeim

1. According to William Sheridan Allen, Spannaus became disenchanted with the Nazi Party after 1933. See William Sheridan Allen, *The Nazi Seizure of Power: The Experience of a Single German Town 1922–1945.* (Franklin Watts, 1984) pp. 27, 32f, 34, 50, 84, 244, 246f, 285, 294, 301f, 308, 334n5. See also Nazis, dissidents.

2. Interview with Mayor Irnfried Rabe and city archivist Ekkehard Just, December 5, 2003.

3. Hans Harer, "Rückkehr in den Tod," *Northeimer Neueste Nachrichten*, January 27, 2005.

4. Author interview with Lotte Seidel (née Oppenheim) March 6, 2005. About Jewish life in Northeim: Iris Vielberg; Gisela Murken; Gerhard Ballin, *Jüdische Mitbürger in Northeim vom späten Mittelalter bis zur Neuzeit* (Northeim: Stadt Northeim, 1988). Author interview by mail with Hans Ballin, a former Jewish resident of Northeim, April 2, 2004.

26. Hannover

1. The letter from Nettchen Stern that describes the suicide of her neighbor Erna Waller was sent on July 3, 1939. Erna Waller died on June 14, 1939. See: Uta Schäfer-Richter, *Die jüdischen Bürger im Kreis Göttingen 1933–1945: Göttingen – Hann. Münden – Duderstadt. Ein Gedenkbuch* (Göttingen: Wallstein, 1992), p. 265.

2. Ahlem. Tour with Martina Mussmann. Tour with Gabriele Lehmberg.

27. Riga

1. Interview with Lore Oppenheimer, September 25, 2005. Interview with Ruth Joffe, October 23, 2003. Interview with Gerda Wasserman, November 28, 2005. Nettchen Stern in Yad Vashem's Central Database of Shoah Victims' Names: https://yvng.yadvashem.org/nameDetails.html?language=en&itemId= 11641757&ind=1 Nettchen Stern in the Memorial book "Victims of the Persecution of Jews under the National Socialist Tyranny in Germany 1933 – 1945" prepared by the German Federal Archives: https://www.bundesarchiv. de/gedenkbuch/en976428

29. "Düsseldorf isn't what it used to be."

1. Thomson, Ian. *Primo Levi: A Life.* (Metropolitan Books, 2014) p. 249 (promotion), 255 (my name is Levi). Gambetta, Diego, "Primo Levi's Last Moments," *Boston Review,* June 1, 1999.
2. For background about Jews in Germany after WWII, see: Lynn Rapaport, *Jews in Germany after the Holocaust: Memory, identity, and Jewish-German relations* (Cambridge: Cambridge University Press, 1997).
3. For information about Friedrich Panse, refer to the notes section for chapter 40.
4. Author email interview with Professor Heinz Häfner, April 15, 2019. About Walter von Baeyer in the Biographical Archive of Psychiatry: https://www. biapsy.de/index.php/en/9-biographien-a-z/84-von-baeyer-walter-ritter-e
Häfner H., "From the catastrophe to a humane mental-health care and successful research in German psychiatry (1951–2012)–as I remember it." Acta Psychiatrica Scandinavica. 2013. June; 127(6):415–32. doi: 10.1111/acps. 12061.

30. Zurich

1. *Shelanu* (or *sche lanu*) in Hebrew means "ours".

32. Tel Aviv

1. War between Israel and Egypt in the Sinai desert (29 October-5 November 1956).

33. Tel Aviv

1. Letters of condolence: Ernst Katzenstein to Lucie Mendel, May 12, 1957. Trude and Hugo Aschenberg to Lucie Mendel, May 14, 1957. Mary and Franz Fürstenberg to Lucie Mendel, April 13, 1957.

2. Announcements of Hugo Mendel's death were published in the following newspapers (in Hebrew): *Haaretz, Herut, Kol Ha'am, Lamerchav*. March 21, 1957, p. 4. *Yediot Aharonot*, March 21, 1957, p. 4.; *The Jerusalem Post*, March 21, 1957, p. 3. Obituary of Hugo Mendel in *Unsere Stimme*, June 1957, by Leo Landau.

34. Tel Aviv

1. *"Herr Jesus noch mal!"*. Literally: Lord Jesus again.

35. Jerusalem

1. Author's multiple interviews with Raphi Medan. The information about Raphi Medan and Fritz Bauer is from Ronen Bergman, "Saying Good-bye to a Hero." July 6, 2017. *Yediot Aharonot* (in Hebrew).
2. The testimonies of Eliezer Karstadt and Benno Cohen during the Eichmann trial are quoted from the trial transcript (in Hebrew): volume A, p. 418, (Karstadt), volume A, p. 182 (Cohen).

37. Tel Aviv

1. Deposition by Lucie Mendel, April 8, 1962.
2. Letter from the office of Hagemann Haumann and Isphording to Dr. Lichtenstein, May 3, 1962.
3. Deposition by Mirjam Rosen, May 24, 1962.
4. Letter from Dr. Lichtenstein to Regierungspräsident Arnsberg (Westf.), May 24, 1962. This material was then forwarded to the *Landesrentenbehörde* (the State Pension Office), which confirmed receipt on July 5, 1962.

38. Zurich

1. Letter from LRB to Lucie Mendel and Dr. Lichtenstein, March 11, 1963. Letter from Dr. Lichtenstein to Lucie Mendel, April 3, 1963.

39. Tel Aviv

1. Letter from Dr. Lichtenstein to the LRB, May 14, 1963. Letter from LRB to Dr. Lichtenstein, May 22, 1963.
2. Letter from Dr. Lichtenstein to Dr. Dahlfeld, August 4, 1963. Letter from Dr. Dahlfeld to Dr. Lichtenstein, August 15, 1963.
3. Court request for expert witness, December 17, 1963.

40. Menlo Park

1. Regarding Friedrich Panse: Author's email correspondence with Dr. Ralf Forsbach, February 2019. R. Forsbach, "Friedrich Panse – etabliert in allen Systemen." *Nervenarzt* (2012) 83: 329. https://doi.org/10.1007/s00115-011-3390-8 Ralf Forsbach, *Die Medizinische Fakultät der Universität Bonn im "Dritten Reich,"* (De Gruyter Oldenbourg, 2006). Christian Pross, *Paying for the Past: The Struggle over Reparations for Surviving Victims of the Nazi Terror* (Baltimore: The Johns Hopkins University Press 1998) pp. 84–85. Biess Frank, *Homecomings: Returning POWs and the Legacies of Defeat in Postwar Germany* (Princeton, NJ: Princeton University Press, 2009) pp. 78–79. From the Biographical Profiles in Psychiatry. https://biapsy.de/index.php/en/9-biographien-a-z/269-panse-friedrich-albert-e (English). https://biapsy.de/index.php/de/9-biographien-a-z/259-panse-friedrich (German). Wikipedia: https://de.wikipedia.org/wiki/Friedrich_Panse (German).
2. Letter from Dahlfeld to the court November 23, 1964.
3. Letter from Dr. Dahlfeld to Dr. Lichtenstein, March 8, 1965 with attached pages 17-20 from Dr. Panse's report from February 8, 1965.

41. Tel Aviv

1. Deposition by Mirjam Rosen, March 13, 1965. Deposition by Else Schweitzer, May 16, 1965. Deposition by Arthur Katz, May 8, 1965.
2. Letter from Dr. Lichtenstein to Dahlfeld, March 19, 1965.
3. Letter from Dahlfeld to the court, April 20, 1965. The names of the lawyers who committed suicide are from Göppinger, Horst, *Die Verfolgung der Juristen jüdischer Abstammung durch den Nationalsozialismus* (Ring-Verlag, Villingen, 1963) pp. 130-137.
4. Letter from Dr. Dahlfeld to Dr. Lichtenstein, May 10, 1965. Dahlfeld attached his letter to the court from the same day. The BGH decision Dahlfeld cited was from February 17, 1965, IV ZR 72/64.
5. Letter from Dahlfeld to Lichtenstein, March 31, 1966.
6. Letter from Dahlfeld to Lichtenstein, June 4, 1965.
7. Letter from Dahlfeld to Lichtenstein, April 7, 1966.
8. Letter from Lichtenstein to Dahlfeld, April 15, 1966.
9. https://www.dgppn.de/die-dgppn/geschichte/chronikderpraesidenten.html (in German).
10. Letter from Landgericht Düsseldorf (the court) to Michels and Dahlfeld, September 28, 1966. Letter from Dahlfeld to Lichtenstein, October 7, 1966.
11. Letter from the LRB to the court on October 21, 1966. Letter from Dahlfeld to Lichtenstein, March 8, 1967. Landgericht Düsseldorf (the court) decision from March 6, 1967. Letter from Dahlfeld to Lichtenstein, October 7, 1966; May 14, 1967.

42. Tel Aviv

1. The LRB to Oberlandesgericht Düsseldorf, July 5, 1967.
2. Dahlfeld to the Oberlandesgericht Düsseldorf, July 19, 1967.
3. Erwin Lichtenstein, *Bericht an meine Familie: ein Leben zwischen Danzig und Israel* (Darmstadt: Luchterhand, 1985) p. 201.
4. Letter from "the office of Dr. Lichtenstein" to Dahlfeld, August 4, 1967.
5. Letter from Dahlfeld to Lichtenstein, December 1, 1967. Court decision from November 29, 1967.
6. Letter from Dr. Lichtenstein to Dahlfeld January 10, 1968.
7. Letter from Dahlfeld to the Oberlandesgericht Düsseldorf, October 3, 1968.

43. Tel Aviv

1. Decision by the Oberlandesgericht Düsseldorf, February 10, 1969. Specialist report by Walter Ritter von Baeyer from September 20, 1968.
2. Decision by the Oberlandesgericht Düsseldorf, October 29, 1969.
3. Hannah Arendt, "We Refugees," *Menorah Journal* 31, no. 1 (January 1943): pp. 69–77. The article also appears in Hannah Arendt, *The Jewish Writings*, Schocken, 2009. p. 264.

Epilogue

1. Letter from M. Glass at the Israeli Ministry of Justice to Mirjam Rosen, August 25, 1980.
2. Source: Biographical Profiles in Psychiatry. https://biapsy.de/index.php/en/9-biographien-a-z/269-panse-friedrich-albert-e (English) https://biapsy.de/index.php/de/9-biographien-a-z/259-panse-friedrich (German) https://www.dgppn.de/die-dgppn/geschichte/chronikderpraesidenten.html (German) The note reads: Aberkennung der Ehrenmitgliedschaft mit Beschluss v. 24.11.2011.

ACKNOWLEDGMENTS

Writing this book was like putting together a jigsaw puzzle, with two exceptions. First, I didn't have all the pieces, and second I didn't have the picture on the box to give me an idea of what the end product will look like. In other words, I was clueless. This is why I'm so thankful to the dozens of people, who each handed me a few pieces of the puzzle and helped me fit them in the right place. These people include (in no particular order): Martin Mendel, Miriam Tolkowsky, Franz Rose, Gertrud Katz, Yael Katz, Idith Althausen, Emmy Bödeker, Beate Bödeker-Kenke, Frank Ephraim, Miriam Loewy, Paul Otto Samuelsdorff, Daniela Samuelsdorff, Miryam Rothenstein, Mechtild Brand, Wolfgang Schriek, Wolfgang Komo, Angelika Lauhus, Richard Müller-Schmitt, Jana Rogge, Michael Katzenstein, Hansjörg Schiebe, Ofer Binheim, Yehudit Binheim, Ruth Grossman, Benjamin Grossman, Irnfried Rabe, Ekkehard Just, Hans Harer, Martina Mussmann, Gabriele Lehmberg, Lore Oppenheimer, Ruth Joffe, Gerda Wasserman, Heinz Häfner, Raphi Medan, Reuven Givon, Michal Heinberg, Michael Eichenberg, Lotte Seidel, Meredith Alexander, Elisabeth Segre, Ralf Forsbach. Yaakov Froelich, Hertha Adler, and Nadine Gaab. I am responsible for the accuracy, clarity, and opinions in this book but I am grateful for the help these people gave me.

In my travels, I visited many libraries and archives and I would like to extend my gratitude to librarians and archivists in Hamm, Frankfurt, Wiesbaden, Northeim, Jerusalem, Tel Aviv, New York and other cities who were always welcoming and so helpful. This also includes those who have labored behind the scenes on posting information in online archives such as the Leo Baeck Institute archive, the Central Zionist Archive, Yad Vashem, Historical Jewish Press, and others.

I am grateful to Liesbeth Heenk at Amsterdam Publishers for turning the manuscript into a real book! And I feel lucky to have worked with Amsterdam Publishers' network of professionals including Heather Rothman. Thanks also to Meredith Alexander for editing an earlier version of the manuscript.

Thanks to Bernhard Schlink, Carla Fine, Gabriela Shalev, W. Michael Blumenthal, and Martha Minow for the kind words. So many other people helped me with words of encouragement and by commenting on early versions of the manuscript and I'm grateful to each and every one of them. There's simply not enough room to list them all, but I must mention my friends and my extended family in Israel who served simultaneously as research assistants, advisors and cheerleaders. At the top of that list is my sister Eva Dimand who has provided me with invaluable help and encouragement from the very beginning of this project. My wife Daria and my children Noam, Yonatan, Maya, and Mika went with me to Germany after my initial research trip and have been with me on this journey ever since. Your questions, encouragement, and support mean everything to me. Thank you.

ABOUT THE AUTHOR

Emanuel (Manu) Rosen is a bestselling author whose books have been translated into thirteen languages. He was born in Israel where he went to school, served in the army, and was an award-winning copywriter. After his graduate school education in the United States and a successful career as an executive in Silicon Valley, Emanuel turned to write.

He is married to Daria Mochly-Rosen, a professor at Stanford. They live in Menlo Park, California, and have four adult children. *If Anyone Calls, Tell Them I Died* is his fourth book.

HOLOCAUST SURVIVOR TRUE STORIES

The Series **Holocaust Survivor True Stories WWII**, by Amsterdam Publishers, consists of the following biographies:

1. Among the Reeds. The true story of how a family survived the Holocaust, by Tammy Bottner

Amazon Link: getbook.at/ATRBottner

2. A Holocaust Memoir of Love & Resilience. Mama's Survival from Lithuania to America, by Ettie Zilber

Amazon Link: getbook.at/Zilber

3. Living among the Dead. My Grandmother's Holocaust Survival Story of Love and Strength, by Adena Bernstein Astrowsky

Amazon Link: mybook.to/ManiaL

4. Heart Songs - A Holocaust Memoir, by Barbara Gilford

Amazon Link: getbook.at/HeartSongs

5. Shoes of the Shoah. The Tomorrow of Yesterday, by Dorothy Pierce

Amazon Link: getbook.at/shoah

6. Hidden in Berlin. A Holocaust Memoir, by Evelyn Joseph Grossman

Amazon Link: getbook.at/HiddenBL

7. If Anyone Calls, Tell Them I Died, by Emanuel (Manu) Rosen

Amazon Link: getbook.at/EMrosen

8. The Man Across the River: The incredible story of one man's will to survive the Holocaust, by Zvi Wiesenfeld

Amazon Link: getbook.at/ZviWi

HOLOCAUST SURVIVOR MEMOIRS

The Series **Holocaust Survivor Memoirs World War II** , by Amsterdam Publishers, consists of the following autobiographies of survivors:

1. Outcry - Holocaust Memoirs, by Manny Steinberg

Amazon Link: getbook.at/Outcry

2. Hank Brodt Holocaust Memoirs. A Candle and a Promise, by Deborah Donnelly

Amazon Link: getbook.at/Brodt

3. The Dead Years. Holocaust Memoirs, by Joseph Schupack

Amazon Link: getbook.at/Schupack

4. Rescued from the Ashes. The Diary of Leokadia Schmidt, Survivor of the Warsaw Ghetto, by Leokadia Schmidt

Amazon Link: getbook.at/Leokadia

5. My Lvov. Holocaust Memoir of a twelve-year-old Girl, by Janina Hescheles

Amazon Link: getbook.at/Lvov

6. Remembering Ravensbrück. From Holocaust to Healing, by Natalie Hess

Amazon Link: getbook.at/Ravensbruck

7. Wolf. A Story of Hate, by Zeev Scheinwald with Ella Scheinwald

Amazon Link: getbook.at/wolf

8. Save my Children. An Astonishing Tale of Survival and its Unlikely Hero, by Leon Kleiner with Edwin Stepp

Amazon Link: getbook.at/LeonKleiner

9. Holocaust Memoirs of a Bergen-Belsen Survivor & Classmate of Anne Frank, by Nanette Blitz Konig

Amazon Link: getbook.at/BlitzKonig

10. Defiant German - Defiant Jew. A Holocaust Memoir from inside the Third Reich, by Walter Leopold with Les Leopold

Amazon Link: getbook.at/leopold

CPSIA information can be obtained
at www.ICGtesting.com
Printed in the USA
LVHW090205150321
681561LV00036B/665/J